Drugs
Should They Be Legalized?

Marilyn Tower Oliver

—Issues in Focus—

Enslow Publishers, Inc.
44 Fadem Road   PO Box 38
Box 699   Aldershot
Springfield, NJ 07081   Hants GU12 6BP
USA   UK

For my father, Archie Lester Tower, an extraordinary attorney who taught me to always consider both sides of any issue.

Copyright © 1996 by Marilyn Tower Oliver

Library of Congress Cataloging-in-Publication Data

Oliver, Marilyn Tower.
    Drugs : should they be legalized? / Marilyn Tower Oliver.
        p. cm. — (Issues in focus)
    Includes bibliographical references and index.
    Summary: Discusses the issues surrounding the controversial idea of legalizing certain types of drugs in the United States.
    ISBN 0-89490-738-7
    1. Drug abuse—United States—Juvenile literature. 2. Drug legalization—United States—Juvenile literature. [1. Drug abuse. 2. Drug legalization. 3. Narcotic laws.] I. Title. II. Series: Issues in focus (Hillside, N.J.)
    HV5825.O53 1996
    362.29'0973—dc20   96-12265
                                                          CIP
                                                          AC

Printed in the United States of America

10 9 8 7 6 5 4 3 2 1

Illustration Credits: Drug Enforcement Administration, pp. 50, 64, 67, 69; Library of Congress, pp. 9, 24, 27, 72, 85; Marilyn Tower Oliver, pp. 73, 77, 93, 113; National Archives, pp. 26, 48, 100, 109; The National Library of Medicine, pp. 15, 18; © Winn Krafton, p. 36.

Cover Illustration: © Winn Krafton

Contents

Acknowledgments

The author would like to thank the following for their time and assistance in helping research this book:
—The Cato Institute, Washington D.C.
—Committees of Correspondence
—Officer George Ducoulombier, Sheriff's Department Information Bureau, Los Angeles County Sheriff's Department
—The Drug Enforcement Administration, John Broehn and Diane Martin, Public Information officers
—Families Against Mandatory Minimums Foundation
—Forfeiture Endangers American Rights (F.E.A.R.), John T. Paff, secretary
—National Organization for the Reform of Marijuana Laws (NORML)
—Bruce Margolin, director NORML, Southern California
—National Institute on Drug Abuse
—National Library of Medicine
—Office of National Drug Control Policy, Executive Office of the President
—Partnership for a Drug Free America
—PRIDE, Inc. Parents' Resource Institute for Drug Education

1

Legalization vs. Regulation: The Issue

Whether or not they use illegal drugs, all students can be affected by the laws that control their use.

In June 1995, the Supreme Court ruled that an Oregon school district had the right to test the urine of school athletes for drugs. The case had been brought by James Acton, a seventh-grade basketball player, and his parents. The Actons objected to the required drug test because James had not used drugs. They believed the drug tests were unconstitutional. The decision of the Court had the potential to open the way for testing millions of students, including nonathletes.

"The state's power over school children . . . permit[s] a degree of supervision and control that could not be exercised over free adults," wrote Justice Antonin Scalia.[1]

In the late 1980s, authorities believed they were winning the war against drugs among young people. News of the dangers of using marijuana and cocaine had made an impact on American youth.

Many felt that the national drug policy, known as the war on drugs, had been a success.

Since 1991, however, drug use seems to have increased among teenagers. In spite of the billions of dollars that have been spent trying to fight drugs and drug abuse, illegal substances still are easy to obtain. Use of alcohol and tobacco, illegal drugs for teens, has also increased. Even children in elementary school are using drugs.

According to 1994 statistics from the American Council for Drug Education, by the fourth grade, 40 percent of students feel pressured to smoke cigarettes; 34 percent may drink wine coolers; and 24 percent say their friends encourage them to try crack or cocaine.[2]

Most people acknowledge that there is a serious drug problem in the United States, but they do not agree on the best ways to deal with it.

Some authorities look with interest at the drug situation in the Netherlands, a country in Europe. There, possession of small amounts of marijuana and hashish is legal and as easy to buy as ice cream or a cup of coffee. The drugs are sold in coffeehouses.

The Dutch do not believe that society can stop people from taking drugs. They believe that the drug crisis is a health problem, not a crime problem. Policing the coffee-shop scene costs them very little money, because they do not believe that crime is associated with the use of marijuana. Allowing young people to experiment with drugs in an open atmosphere keeps them from associating with drug dealers who might introduce them to hard drugs.

Not prosecuting the small user means the Dutch officials can spend more money enforcing laws against drug dealers, traffickers, and organized crime.

Marijuana is not the only legal drug in the Netherlands. Addicts can buy and sell up to half a gram of heroin, cocaine, or amphetamines and the police will look the other way.

Are there more drug users in the Netherlands? "Statistics show that this policy works because the number of hard drug users has stabilized for more than 10 years," said Rob Hessing, chief of police of the Dutch city of Rotterdam.

"A lot of users are not criminals. They are working, have a job, are not unemployed. What we fight against is the dealers, the traffickers, the organized crime, and very hard. We don't hunt the users," said Chief of Police Hessing in a television interview with ABC newscaster Catherine Crier.[3]

Drug abuse is a serious problem in the United States. On the street, illegal drugs represent tens of billions of dollars each year. The social costs are also high—crime, AIDS, crack-addicted babies, prison overcrowding, urban decay.

Even though the United States spends billions of dollars to fight the war on drugs, they still seem to be readily available. More Americans are also behind bars for drug use. Some are dangerous, high-level drug dealers. Most, however, are nonviolent users who have no criminal records except for being caught in possession of a small quantity of drugs. Of the approximately seven hundred fifty thousand people arrested for drugs every year, three fourths are there for possession, creating overcrowded prisons.[4]

Jim Montgomery is an example. He is a forty-one-year-old paraplegic who was convicted of possession with intent to distribute two ounces of marijuana, about the same amount as the tobacco in two packs of cigarettes. The police found the marijuana in his wheelchair. Montgomery said that he smokes the drug to help relieve the pain from his broken back. In the United States, it is illegal to possess marijuana for medical purposes without special permission.

A jury gave him a sentence of life in prison, but he is serving a reduced sentence of ten years, a longer sentence than the average time served for murder in the United States.[5]

Some people believe that we need to examine our drug laws to see if they help solve the problem of drug abuse and drug trafficking or if they contribute to it. They point to the parallels between the prohibition of alcohol between 1917 and 1933, which caused an increase in crime and violence, and the current prohibitions against illegal drugs. They argue that legalizing drugs will eliminate the drug lords, the violence, and the profits from the illegal trade. The money saved could be spent on antidrug education and treatment for addicts, they say.

On the other hand, many others support the present policy which prohibits drugs. They believe that legalization would open the door to increased drug use, which would cause severe health and crime problems. Legalizing drugs would make them cheaper and would create more addicts who would commit more crimes. Because

In the nineteenth century, illegal manufacture of alcohol was considered more serious than selling some drugs. In the South, the army would seek out underground stills where bootleg or "moonshine" liquor was being made.

drugs would still be illegal for minors, young people would become the target market for drug pushers.[6]

Illegal, dangerous drugs must be tightly controlled, they say. They are particularly concerned about statistics that point to greater drug use among junior high and senior high school students. To discourage drug use, some advocate mandatory minimum sentences for drug possession and drug dealing. They would continue to ban any drug use.

Groups such as National Families in Action, an

organization opposed to the legalization of drugs, point to alcohol and tobacco, two drugs that are legal for adults. Because alcohol and tobacco are easy to obtain, ten Americans use alcohol and five use tobacco for every American who uses illegal drugs. Opponents to legalization believe that if other drugs were legalized, more people would use them, more would become addicted, and more would die.[7]

Many people who favor some form of legalization support cracking down on drug lords and drug trafficking. They are concerned, however, that in spite of the billions of dollars spent to combat drugs, the drug problem is still with us. Drugs such as crack are openly sold on the street. Rival gangs shoot at each others over drug turf wars, and innocent people are murdered in the cross fire.

Legalization of drugs is a very complex issue. Many politicians want to appear tough on drugs because they believe that a majority of their constituents are opposed to legalization. In many cases, courts have upheld mandatory drug testing, search and seizure laws, and laws against selling drug paraphernalia.

A majority of Americans seems to agree. "You will never persuade the citizens of this country—never—that they should legalize drugs," said former drug policy administrator ("drug czar") William Bennett.[8]

Up to 1914, however, many of the drugs that are illegal now were legal in the United States. Let's take a look at the history of drug use and abuse in the world and in America.

2

Drugs Have Always Been a Part of Society

Drugs have been around since the beginning of recorded history. Most of the time they have been legal. Only in this century have they been illegal.

Drugs in the Ancient World

More than five thousand years ago, the ancient Sumerians, a people who lived in the area now known as Iraq, cultivated a type of poppy that they called "joy plant." The juice they extracted from the poppies was dried to produce opium, a powerful narcotic which reduces pain and causes sleep. The drug has been used through the ages as a medicine and as a recreational drug. (A recreational drug is one that is taken to change one's mood, rather than for a medical reason.)

Jars of opium have also been found in Egyptian tombs. Tutankhamen, better known as King Tut, was a boy-king who became ruler of Egypt around 1334 B.C.

He is famous because of the richness of his tomb. During King Tut's reign, the Egyptians carried on a prosperous trade in opium, which they called spenn, throughout the Middle East. Egyptian doctors were probably the first to prescribe a small dose of opium to calm crying babies. Between 1600 and 600 B.C., the tombs of the pharaohs were often decorated with paintings of opium poppies.[1]

Opium was not the only drug known in the ancient world. The Scythians were an ancient people who lived in a region near the Black Sea, near modern-day Turkey.

The historian Herodotus of Halikarnassus wrote that the Sythians would place a dish filled with red-hot coals in a small tent made by stretching strips of woolen cloth on a framework of three sticks. They would place hemp seeds (marijuana) on the coals. Then they inhaled the smoke. "The Scythians enjoy it so much that they howl with pleasure," Herodotus wrote.[2]

In the Andean highlands of South America, indigenous people have long chewed the leaves of the coca plant to help them endure the cold climate and hunger. Coca leaves can be processed into cocaine. Inca priests in Peru used coca to throw themselves into a religious trance so that they could predict the future.[3]

Drugs of the Middle Ages

Throughout the Middle Ages, in Europe, the opium poppy was known as a painkiller, but it was hard to obtain. By the eighteenth century, there was debate over the use of opium. Scientists engaged in clinical research to find out more about the drug.

In Germany, a sixteen-year-old pharmacist's helper named Friedrich Sertuerner was determined to isolate the active ingredient in the juice of the opium poppy. After four years of experiments, he was able to extract white crystals, or alkaloids. Because the crystals caused patients to go to sleep, he called this drug morphine after Morpheus, the Greek god of dreams.

When Sertuerner tested the drug on three local teenagers, a scandal broke out, and he was forced to stop his research.[4]

Early Drug Use in America

In the United States, the opinions about drug use have swung from acceptance to disapproval.

Although drugs such as opium, morphine, heroin, cocaine, and marijuana are illegal in the United States today, in the nineteenth century, they were used as medicines and as tonics. Today, using, buying, selling, or possessing most of these drugs is considered a crime. Morphine and cocaine can only be used if they are prescribed by a doctor.

At the early part of the nineteenth century, opium and morphine were used to help reduce pain and to promote well-being.

Although opium came from Turkey and Asia, its popularity at the beginning of the nineteenth century led one Baltimore doctor to suggest that home gardeners cultivate opium poppies for medicinal use as well as for the beauty of the plant.

The poppies were grown in Virginia, Georgia, Tennessee, South Carolina, Louisiana, Arizona Territory,

13

and California as well as in other states. One writer even suggested that small monkeys could be trained to tend the opium poppy crops in California. The cost of growing the poppies in the United States, however, was not competitive with the cost of crops from Turkey and the Middle East.[5]

As the century passed, several forms of opium became familiar. It was usually prescribed as a medicine, most often appearing in solutions. When mixed with alcohol and water it was called laudanum. When opium was combined with camphor, a medicine distilled from the wood and bark of the camphor tree, it created a drug called paregoric, which was used to calm infants and to stop dysentery, an illness that produces severe diarrhea.

A medicine called "Mrs. Winslow's Soothing Syrup," which contained 10 percent morphine, the principal component of opium, was widely used to sooth infants suffering from teething pain.[6]

Because of its ability to reduce pain, opium and its derivative, morphine, were widely used to relieve the suffering of injury victims. By the Civil War, in the 1860s, some doctors were warning their patients about the addictive qualities of morphine, but other physicians did not believe that the drug was addictive and continued to prescribe it.

During the nineteenth century, many people were worried about the dangers of becoming addicted to opium. They called the people who used opium "opium eaters." An article in the *Boston Medical and Surgical Journal* in 1838 stated that opium addicts rarely reached the age of forty. The article described the symptoms of

Mrs. Winslow's Soothing Syrup, a popular nonprescription medicine that eased the pain of teething in babies and young children, was easy to obtain in the nineteenth century.

opium use—a yellow appearance, a bent spine, deep-sunken eyes, and a loss of mental ability.[7]

Some critics began to call for laws to control opium and morphine use. At the same time, patent medicines, many containing opium products, were becoming popular. A patent medicine bears a trademark and can be purchased without a prescription. These drugs were easily obtained at pharmacies and through mail order.

The Search for New Painkillers

Through the latter part of the nineteenth century, there was a continued interest in discovering new drugs to help fight pain. Often these products were enthusiastically received without the testing that drugs

15

undergo today. It was only after the drugs were widely used that some were discovered to be addictive.

This was the case with chloroform and ether, two painkilling drugs. When these drugs were first introduced in the late 1840s, they were used as anesthetics to relieve the pain of surgery and dentistry. Soon they were being abused. By the 1850s, using them to get high had become a fad that was especially popular with medical and dental students, who could easily obtain the drugs. Getting high with these drugs was called a "jag." These drugs were also a rage in high society because their use did not cause a hangover. The drugs caused a feeling of calmness. Although chloroform and ether were not addictive drugs, doctors did warn against their use because overdosing could cause death.[8] Today, these drugs are still used in medicine.

The introduction of a new drug, chloral hydrate, at first met with praise. The drug was invented by a German scientist in 1869, and it was said to give relief from insomnia, the inability to sleep. Like morphine and chloroform, chloral hydrate was easily purchased in drug stores. The drug spread like wildfire.

One superintendent of an insane asylum was so enthusiastic about the drug that he suggested serving patients a bedtime drink of chloral hydrate, eggnog, and whisky.

Enthusiasm for the drug was premature. Within a few decades, doctors noticed that people who used these drugs often suffered from reduced mental power and personality changes.

Chloral hydrate also appeared to be habit-forming. It was noticed that the drug played a part in suicides and accidental deaths. It is interesting to note that chloral hydrate was not a street drug. At the height of the drug's popularity, it was used by businesspeople, teachers, and other leaders of society.[9]

Cocaine and Cannabis

At the midpoint of the nineteenth century, the coca leaf was relatively unknown except to some pharmacists and travelers. By the late 1850s, European chemists isolated the plant's main ingredient and called it cocaine. It was not well known in America until 1877 when it was described in an article in the *Boston Medical and Surgical Journal.*

People were not aware of the differences between coca leaves, which were less powerful, and the derivative cocaine, which was much stronger.

Cocaine was considered helpful for the symptoms of hay fever and as a cure for opium, morphine, and alcohol addiction. William Hammond, former surgeon general of the army, drank a wineglass full of cocaine with every meal and endorsed cocaine as the official remedy of the Hay Fever Association. The psychiatrist Sigmund Freud also praised the drug as a tonic and addiction cure.[10]

Cocaine was added to several popular beverages. John Pemberton, a liver-pill merchant, experimented with extracts from coca leaves, caffeine from the kola nut, and wine to make a beverage he called Coca-Cola®. In 1906, the United States government ordered the manufacturer to take the coca leaf extract out of the drink.[11]

In the nineteenth century, a glass of Vin Mariani taken before or after meals was thought to be a healthful, energy-producing drink. Vin Mariani was one of several popular drinks that contained Peruvian coca.

By the end of the nineteenth century, cocaine's popularity in medicine had declined, partly because newer and more effective painkillers had come on the market. It was still used by some doctors as a local painkiller, and it could still be easily bought at drugstores. It was criticized for causing users to become violent.[12]

In some states where alcohol was forbidden, cocaine was used as a substitute. It was even peddled door to door. In the early 1900s, some states wrote laws to stop these practices. It was believed that federal laws against cocaine would be unconstitutional.[13]

Products from another plant, cannabis, were also available in candy and some drinks. The drugs hashish and marijuana come from this plant. As a medical drug, cannabis was used to treat illnesses such as venereal disease, headaches, and insomnia. In the nineteenth century, physicians did not have many medicines to treat these disorders.

With time, however, doctors began to mistrust cannabis because it was unpredictable. Like cocaine, it sometimes would make users appear irrational and mentally disturbed. By 1900, some critics cautioned that large doses of cannabis could lead to violence or insanity.[14]

The False Promise of Heroin

There was great excitement in 1898 when the Bayer Company in Germany began to market a new opiate based on morphine. An opiate is a medicine containing opium. The drug was named heroin because it was thought to be heroic in its ability to cure. The drug's supporters believed that it was not habit forming. Some doctors even thought that it would be useful in treating morphine addicts.

Soon heroin began to appear in over-the-counter medicines, especially in products for coughs and congestion, asthma, and bronchitis.

By 1910, however, there were serious concerns about the addictive qualities of the drug. People were using the drug to cause feelings of well-being. A neighborhood in Boston where heroin was openly sold was called Heroin

19

Square. In Philadelphia, it was reported that one druggist bought twenty-five thousand heroin tablets.

Most of the heroin users were young white males who lived in cities. Like users today, they robbed and stole to finance their drug use. Many people viewed with alarm the fact that these young men seemed to form sub-cultures or gangs that did not want to contribute to society.[15]

Concerns About Addiction

In the nineteenth and early twentieth centuries, many people were concerned about drug addiction, but they could not agree on how to treat it. One problem was that doctors disagreed about the causes of addiction. Addicts knew that willpower alone was not enough to solve their addictions. Many looked for cures, but they found that stopping drug use was a painful process. During withdrawal, the addict might experience diarrhea, vomiting, discharges from the mucous membranes, muscle pain, and sensitive skin. Unable to cope with the pain, users often returned to drug use.

Some people were so desperate for a cure that they would buy mail-order drugs that claimed they would help an addict control his or her addiction. These ineffective potions would be mailed in brown paper wrapping so that neighbors and family would not know that an addict was in their midst. Rather than helping, many patent medicines would add to an addict's problems because many contained alcohol, cocaine, or morphine.

In the 1880s, cocaine was thought of as a substitute

for opium because it did not produce physical dependence. When some patients became psychologically dependent on cocaine, it lost popularity.

Until they were found to be addictive, heroin and codeine (a milder drug which is also produced from opium) were used to fight opium addiction.[16]

Calls for Regulation

By the early 1900s, there was a movement toward regulation of drugs, fueled in part by the debate over cocaine and heroin.

When cocaine was first introduced, it appealed to people who wanted to have high energy to accomplish socially acceptable work. When the drug became popular with young people and with what was considered as the criminal element, it was viewed with more alarm. Pure food and drug supporters tried to have coca removed from popular drinks.[17]

Heroin use also caused fears that a drug subculture would cause users to reject society. "The addicts become late and irregular in their hours of work and finally they throw up their positions. Many are good workmen, but they only work long enough to procure money with which to buy the drug," said Sarah Graham-Mulhall, a reformer in the early 1920s who wanted to regulate the drug.[18]

Racism also entered into the picture when people began to associate drug use with minorities, especially African Americans and Chinese. In 1909, Congress passed a law banning the sale of opium. The new law targeted Chinese as well as gamblers and prostitutes.[19]

In 1906, Congress passed the District of Columbia Pharmacy Act. This regulated the nonmedical use of opiates, cocaine, and chloral hydrate in the District. Doctors were required to write an order to renew a narcotic prescription, and they were forbidden to prescribe narcotics to maintain a patient's addiction.[20]

The year 1906 also saw the formation of the Pure Food and Drug Act, which required manufacturers of opium-based drugs to list the ingredient on the label.[21]

The Father of American Narcotics Laws

Dr. Hamilton Wright, a reformer, is considered to be the father of American narcotic laws. He was a leader in the drive for international drug control after 1900 and became a leader in the international war against opium. Wright believed that the United States had a major drug problem, and he decided to investigate it. In 1908, he conducted a survey by writing hundreds of letters to doctors, pharmacists, and drug importers in an attempt to see how much opium-related drugs and cocaine were being used as medicine and how much was being channeled to other uses. His survey uncovered the fact that much of the drugs imported into the United States were not being used medically. Wright and other reformers later used these results to build public support for drug control.[22]

Wright also helped focus attention on the international drug problem. An employee of the State Department, Wright came up with the idea that it was in the interest of the United States to gain favor with China in order to be able to trade with that country.

China had a serious problem with opium. Wright believed that if the United States could help China control its opium trade, China would look favorably on doing business with the United States.[23]

The opium problem in China dated back to the early nineteenth century when Portuguese and British traders began to introduce the drug there. Opium was grown in Southeast Asia in countries under the authority of Great Britain. These traders believed that they could profit from encouraging the Chinese to use the drug. They also wanted to force China to open its ports to trading with European nations.

The Chinese did not want to expose their people to opium. In 1729, the drug had been banned by imperial law.

China's desire to keep opium out of their country led to the first Opium War with Britain (1839–1842). As a result of this war, China was forced to expand trade and surrender Hong Kong to British rule. A second Opium War (1856–1858) opened more Chinese ports. Opium was brought in through these ports and addiction increased.[24]

Dr. Wright went around the United States speaking before civic and trade groups, championing the idea that American know-how would help solve China's opium problem. The United States proposed the idea of international control of the narcotics trade as a way of getting a leadership role in the Far East. An international opium commission met in Shanghai, China, in 1909. Delegates came from the United States, China, France, Germany, Great Britain, Holland, Italy, Japan, Austria-Hungary, Persia, Portugal, Russia, and Siam (Thailand).

Although China tried to keep opium out of the country, many Chinese became addicted to the drug. By 1900, there were approximately 90 million opium addicts in China.

Later, Wright wrote, "Our move to help China in her opium reform gave us more prestige in China than any of our recent friendly acts toward her. . . . China will recognize that we are sincere in her behalf, and the whole business may be used as oil to smooth the troubled water of our aggressive commercial policy there."[25]

In 1911, a second conference took place in The Hague, Netherlands. The following year, a treaty called The Hague Convention of 1912 was signed into law by thirty-four nations that agreed to control narcotics. The treaty condemned recreational use of opium and stated that the drug should only be used as a medicine. Each nation agreed on how much opium it would import or export.[26]

Although the United States had been a leader in setting up the international control of narcotics, there was not any regulation of drugs in America. This led the delegates to The Hague Convention to push for a law to restrict cocaine and opium in the United States.

The Harrison Narcotics Act

In 1914, the Harrison Act, the first federal drug regulation, passed Congress and was signed into law, taking effect in March 1915. The new law required people who dealt in opium-based drugs to register and to buy tax stamps.

The Harrison Act was designed to regulate, not abolish, drugs. The law did not include cannabis or chloral hydrate, and it did not forbid over-the-counter medicines that contained small amounts of narcotics. Small amounts of cocaine and opium could still be sold without prescriptions, and doctors and dentists could still prescribe the drugs to patients.[27]

As the First World War drew to a close, public sentiment reflected a disgust with all types of addiction. Drug and alcohol use was viewed as a moral weakness. In 1919, passage of the Eighteenth Amendment created Prohibition, which forbid the sale of alcohol. The Volstead Act, passed by Congress over President Woodrow

In America, opium dens such as this one created a public demand for stiffer laws against drugs. In 1912, delegates to The Hague Convention pushed for a law to restrict the use of cocaine and opium in the United States.

Wilson's veto, provided the legislation that allowed for the enforcement of Prohibition.[28]

In 1919, Congress amended the Harrison Act to make the possession of regulated drugs without a tax stamp illegal.

The legality of the Harrison Act was upheld by the Supreme Court in 1919 in its decisions in two cases. The case of *U.S.* v. *Doremus* involved a doctor in San Antonio, Texas, who had prescribed a large quantity of opiates to addicts. In the case of *Webb et al.* v. *U.S.*, a

In 1919, the passage of the Eighteenth Amendment to the Constitution created Prohibition, which forbade the sale of alcohol. Here, federal agents break up kegs of bootleg alcohol.

pharmacist and a practicing doctor had violated the Harrison Narcotic Act by providing morphine to an addict to maintain his habit. The court decision in these two cases in favor of the government made it illegal for doctors to prescribe narcotics for drug maintenance.[29]

There were calls for even stricter regulation of drugs. In 1921, the Treasury Department, which was responsible for the Harrison Act, organized a Narcotic Division of the Prohibition Unit. This organization controlled drug regulation until 1930 when the Federal Bureau of Narcotics was formed. The number of federal agents was relatively small—170 in 1920, growing to an average of 270 agents during the 1930s.[30]

Harry J. Anslinger was named Commissioner of Narcotics in 1930 and remained in that position until 1962. He supervised the regulation of narcotics in the United States.

Anslinger was a strong supporter of using law enforcement to stop the drug trade. He encouraged the federal war on drugs by tightening the controls against drug smuggling. He believed that drying up supplies would force both dealers and users out into the open where they would be sent to hospitals or prison.[31]

Through the 1930s, the statistics of the Bureau of Narcotics showed that the number of known addicts had declined. Anslinger reported that there were between fifty thousand and sixty thousand known addicts in the United States. This was far fewer than the two hundred fifty thousand to three hundred thousand reported at the turn of the century. The tough regulations seemed to be working.[32]

Critics said that there were more drug users than the

numbers showed. Many people who were not drug suppliers or hard-core visible addicts also used drugs. These might be ordinary people who would take an opiate to cure a headache or other painful condition.[33]

The public viewed drug addicts as criminals and loafers who stole to support their habits. In addition, some jazz musicians, artists, and movie stars used drugs such as cocaine, cannabis, and opium.[34]

In the 1950s, illegal drug use seemed contained in the fringes of society. Most concern involved the growing use of heroin. The stereotype of a drug user was a white or black male teenager or juvenile delinquent, usually living in a city.[35]

Drug Use Increases in the 1960s

During the 1960s attitudes toward drug use changed. Many middle-class youth were rebelling against the rules of society. They questioned and sometimes rejected the customs of society in their actions and their dress. (Some of these young people were called Hippies.) Others protested the war in Vietnam. One of the ways they rejected the values of middle-class society was to seriously experiment with drugs, especially marijuana. By the late 1960s, marijuana use had increased dramatically.

Experimentation with marijuana also was widespread among the military in Vietnam. Approximately half of the soldiers who served in Vietnam also used other drugs, and a fifth returned addicted. The soldiers mirrored the rebellion or revolution against society that was going on at home. To meet the demand for marijuana, some South Vietnamese businesspeople began to grow marijuana to sell to the American troops. The United

States military, alarmed about this situation, began to police the use of marijuana. This crackdown resulted in many soldiers turning to heroin, which was cheap and available. It was reported in 1971 that 10 to 15 percent of American enlisted soldiers were using heroin.[36]

In 1971, President Nixon responded to public worries about the drug problem by declaring a war against drugs.

The fifty-five drug laws already in existence were united into the Controlled Substance Act, known as the CSA. The Commission on Marijuana and Drug Abuse was established.[37]

Two years later, the commission made public their recommendations. Among their suggestions was decriminalization of marijuana. Although marijuana was still illegal, users would be fined rather than arrested for possession of small quantities of pot. President Nixon did not follow this recommendation. The commission also suggested that a single federal agency be created to direct the fight against drugs.

Although the federal government did not decriminalize marijuana, during the 1970s a number of states did move to decriminalize that drug.[38] In 1973, Oregon adopted the idea of decriminalization. Other states followed: Ohio, Alaska, Colorado, Maine, California, Minnesota, Mississippi, North Carolina, New York, and Nebraska. This policy did not mean acceptance of marijuana. Although the laws varied from state to state, decriminalization generally meant that possession or use of a small amount of marijuana was a misdemeanor, a lesser crime than a felony. Possessing a larger quantity, growing the drug, or selling it were still considered serious offenses.[39]

The War on Drugs

In the 1980s, presidents Reagan and Bush both launched an attack on the drug problem. Vast sums of money were spent on the war on drugs. In 1981, the annual budget for the war on drugs was $1.46 billion. In 1992, it was close to $12 billion, an increase of 700 percent.[40]

The number of people who use drugs occasionally has gone down, but the number of addicts has increased or remained the same.

The cost to society has also gone up. In some cities, drug dealing has caused an increase in violent crimes such as drive-by shootings as dealers fight over turf. Often, innocent people are shot. It is claimed that drug dealing also contributes to the decay of neighborhoods.

There are also other concerns. Drug use leads to serious mental and physical problems. Many people fear drug addicts because they believe that they are destroying their minds and are unable to control their actions. Addicts are considered a threat to society.

Some experts, however, argue that drugs are a symptom rather than a cause of social problems. They say that it is unfair to blame drugs for the problems of society.

3

How Serious is the Drug Problem?

Almost everyone agrees that drug abuse is a problem, but there is disagreement about how serious an issue it really is. In the twentieth century, drug use appears to have increased both in the United States and in other industrialized countries around the world.

The U.S. Department of Justice statistics show that in 1900 there were approximately two hundred fifty thousand drug abusers out of a population of 76 million in the United States.

By 1991, there were about 16 million abusers out of a population of 250 million—a 20 percent increase. The same year, approximately 26 million people said they had used drugs.

Do these people pose a threat to society? Many believe that they do. To deal with the problem of drug abuse, state and federal governments have turned to stiffer laws against the sale and use of narcotics and other illegal substances. There are now more than three hundred thirty thousand Americans behind bars for violating drug laws. In spite of the sterner laws, it appears that drug dealing and abuse are still serious problems.

Drug dealers and abusers are not the only ones affected by the rise in drugs. Many people believe that drugs are responsible for much of what they see is wrong with our country. They blame drugs for the decay of parts of our cities. They blame drugs for failures in our schools. They hold drugs responsible for the breakdown of families. They say drugs are responsible for loss of productivity. Drugs, they say, can lead to death.

The 26th Annual Gallup Poll of the Public's Attitude Toward the Public Schools, conducted in 1994, revealed that among the 1,326 adults polled, 78 percent believed that increased use of alcohol and drugs among school-aged youth was a major cause of school violence.[1]

Urban decay, family breakdown, and school violence are complicated issues. While drugs may be partly or even largely responsible, critics say that there are other causes for these problems.

They say that keeping drugs illegal may even be a cause for much of the violence that seems to plague our country. Much of the violence, they say, is due to territorial fights or disputes over drug possession. They believe that removing the profit from drug trafficking would eliminate much of the violence related to drug dealing.

Most people believe that drug use and abuse are serious problems both for the users and for society. They do not all agree, however, on the severity of the problem. How much danger do illegal drugs present in our society?

Let's explore both sides of this complicated question.

Drugs Cause Serious Problems

Drugs do play a role in juvenile delinquency and crime. Take the example of Gallo, a juvenile delinquent who got his nickname from the name of a popular wine. He was only four years old when his brothers introduced him to marijuana.

His pot smoking increased when he was six. That year his brothers also introduced him to cigarettes. By the age of eight, he was also drinking alcohol at family gatherings.

Gallo started using hashish when he was nine, and graduated to harder drugs such as amphetamines, Quaaludes (a tranquilizer), and LSD in his early teens.

About this time he began his criminal career. With friends he would steal cars for joyrides, steal from houses, and deal drugs. Before he was sixteen, he had firebombed a house and assaulted a police officer.

As a teen, he discussed his life history with a social worker. "Everyone was doing it around me, so why shouldn't I?" he asked.[2]

Although a variety of factors may have been involved in Gallo's road to delinquency, drugs played a big part.

Of course, not every drug user goes on to criminal activity, but statistics show that many criminals have drug habits.

The National Institute of Justice Drug Use Forecasting Program studies drug use among arrested prisoners by means of urine tests. The tests are voluntary. The prisoners do not give their names. In twenty-four cities studied in 1992, 42 to 79 percent of male arrestees tested positive for any drug. Positive drug tests for female arrestees were between 38 and 85 percent. Those most likely to test positive were males arrested for drug sale or possession and females charged with prostitution. Prisoners of both sexes arrested for burglary and robbery also had high positive rates.[3]

Drug users often commit crimes against innocent victims to get money or goods to sell to support their drug habits.

In a 1991 survey, 17 percent of state prison inmates reported that they committed their offenses to get money to buy drugs. Offenders convicted of robbery, burglary, and larceny or theft were most likely to commit their offense to get money for drugs.[4]

Drug abuse also tears down many urban neighborhoods and appears to be related to the problems of homelessness. In Skid Row, a downtown area of Los Angeles, where a large number of people live on the streets, it is estimated that 15 percent of the homeless people use cocaine.

In other neighborhoods with large populations of homeless people, the problem may be more serious.

Mike Neely, a former addict who runs a Skid Row outreach program, believes that at least half of the homeless population uses crack cocaine. Other addicts insist that the numbers are much higher—perhaps 70 to 80 percent. Middle-class communities also are affected by drugs.

An example is Santa Monica, a beach city near Los Angeles. Of the eighty-seven thousand residents, the one thousand street people account for one third of police calls and up to 45 percent of bookings in jail. Some

In the poorest areas of downtown Los Angeles where many people live on the streets, it is estimated that 15 percent of the homeless use cocaine or some other drug. Others believe that at least half of the homeless use crack cocaine.

citizens believe that many of these crimes are related to drugs.

"At some parks, they've taken the doors off the bathrooms because of drugs. You never know if a drug deal's going on in the bathrooms," said Jean Sedillos, a member of Save Our City, a group that wants to clean up the parks.[5]

Of the destruction caused by crack cocaine, *Los Angeles Times* reporter Jesse Katz wrote:

> Swarming legions of peddlers, brazenly parading their wares, have become fixtures of a bleak curbside market place, flagging down cars and

pouncing on customers everywhere from the meanest Pico-Union tenement to the farthest corner of the San Fernando Valley. Night and day, hawking and haggling and hustling, they turn residential streets into open-air drug bazaars, verdant parks into treacherous battlefields, abandoned buildings into fetid smoke houses.[6]

Drug use can also lead to child abuse, neglect, and domestic violence.

Charles C. was learning to operate construction equipment in Bakersfield, California, when he became addicted to crack cocaine. Within four months his habit was costing him three hundred dollars a day. He quit school and sold his possessions to buy the drug. When the money ran out, he turned to burglary and armed robbery to get money for his habit. He went to prison, then ended up on Skid Row. He went into treatment after he tried to hang his girlfriend in a drunken rage.

"The drug and alcohol, mixed together just sent me off into a rage," he said. "My life was unmanageable. You want it so much, you're willing to take a chance on losing your life to go out there and get it."[7]

Crack is only one of the drugs that causes problems. Nikki, twenty-three, attended a liberal-arts college in the Northeast. Louise, twenty-nine, is a successful novelist. Susan, twenty-two, has worked as a social worker. For these young women, heroin is the drug of choice.

Drug treatment experts say they have seen a rise in heroin use in the 1990s. They say the new addicts are different from the lower-class people who used the drug in the past.

"Now we are seeing people who are employed, who

are much more socially stable in many ways than the classical picture of the seventies heroin addict," said Anne Geller, a Manhattan physician.[8]

Heroin produces both a psychological and a physical dependence that is very hard to break.

"The problem with heroin is that you become disinterested in what you are doing, and isolate yourself with an I-don't-care, everyone-is-an-idiot attitude," Nikki said.[9]

Marijuana is often the first drug that young users try. Although opinions vary on how dangerous marijuana is, many researchers and youth workers feel that the drug has serious consequences for young users.

"Younger children, at eighth-grade level and below, are at greater risk because their personalities haven't developed well enough, and they aren't mature enough to know how to handle altered states of consciousness. As with any drug, the younger the age of first use, the higher the risk," said Dr. Larry Chair, an independent researcher who has been studying marijuana's effects on human behavior for ten years.[10]

LSD is another drug that has serious effects on users both young and old. The dangers are particularly serious for youth.

"The younger you are the more likely you are to impair your psychosocial development and have adverse reactions," said Dr. David Smith, founder of the Haight-Ashbury Free Clinics in San Francisco.[11]

Statistics show that use of LSD among young people has been rising in recent years. In 1993, 6.8 percent of high school seniors reported using the drug. This is the highest level since 1985. Among eighth graders, 3.5

percent said they had used LSD at least once, up from 2.7 percent in 1991. Drug educators believe that this is a significant increase.[12]

Drug abusers cause problems for themselves and for others. Often they sell drugs to others to help support their habits. Young drug abusers may cause disturbances at school, making it difficult for others to learn. They require expensive treatment to help them control or break their drug habits. An adult user's family may have to go on welfare if the user is not able to keep a job.

Billions of dollars must be spent to control the crimes related to drug trafficking. In 1993, the budget for the Drug Enforcement Agency was nearly $892 million.[13] Local and state law enforcement efforts, courts, and prisons account for even more money. It is estimated that the total cost of drug-related law enforcement is about $10 billion each year. Drug dealers and addicts clog the courts and prisons.

Drug money also contributes to corrupting law enforcement officials. Corruption charges have been made against United States Customs inspectors, FBI agents, police officers, prison guards, and even prosecutors.

In April 1994, in New York City, twenty-nine police officers in the 30th Precinct in Harlem were arrested for stealing drugs and cash from local dealers. This was not the first time officers had gotten into trouble over drugs in the New York area. In 1992, several Brooklyn officers were arrested for staging drug raids and stealing drugs and money from suspects and from crack houses.

Officers have been arrested for similar crimes in other major cities—New Orleans, Miami, and Washington, D.C.[14]

Customs agents who patrol the borders have also been arrested for helping drug traffickers to bring drugs into the United States. In 1995, in El Paso, Texas, two inspectors were charged with conspiring to smuggle 2,200 pounds of cocaine across the border. They received a payoff of $1 million from the smugglers. Eight present and former employees of the U.S. Customs Service in San Diego were charged with helping the Mexican drug cartels to ship tons of cocaine across the United States border at San Diego, California.[15]

Drug-Addicted Babies

The drug user is not the only person to be affected by drug use. Perhaps the saddest consequence of drug abuse is the effect on the innocent—the children and babies of addicts.

Babies born to crack mothers have documented risks of low birth weight, high death rate, and hyperactivity. Later, when they go to school, these children may have emotional and learning problems that affect their behavior.

A Boston study of the children of women who were long-term drug users found that 14 percent of cocaine-exposed two-year-olds were slow to develop. Three- and four-year-olds in the study had a low attention span and trouble with speech.

Cocaine and crack are not the only drugs that can cause difficulties for babies and young children. In the same study, 27 percent of two-year-olds who had been exposed to other drugs before birth had problems with delayed development.[16]

Communities must also pay a high price for drug-addicted babies. In 1988, the medical costs for drug-exposed babies came to $81 million in Los Angeles County. Nationally, it is estimated that the cost to all levels of government to prepare drug babies to enter kindergarten will soon reach $15 billion a year.[17]

Crack mothers also tend to have difficulty bonding with their babies. If the baby is hospitalized, the mothers visit them less often. "When they do come, they are less likely to hold or become involved with their babies," said Dr. Barry Phillips, director of the intensive-care nursery at Children's Hospital in Oakland.[18]

The Seriousness of the Drug Problem May Be Exaggerated

Although drug abuse is a serious issue in the United States, some researchers believe that the problem is exaggerated. They say that although teenagers are exposed to illegal drugs, only a minority actually use drugs regularly.

The 1994 High School Senior Survey of 15,929 public and private high school seniors reported that 21.9 percent had used an illegal drug during the past month. Nineteen percent had used marijuana or hashish, 2.7 percent had tried inhalants, 3.1 percent had used hallucinogens, 2.3 percent had used cocaine or crack, and 2.6 percent had tried LSD. A much higher percentage had used alcohol and tobacco during the month before the survey. Although it is illegal for juveniles to use these substances, they are sold legally in our society: 30.8 percent reported being drunk, and 31.2 percent had smoked cigarettes.[19]

41

Alcohol is a legal drug for adults that alters human behavior. It creates serious problems in our society. In 1989, there were an estimated 100 million users of alcohol in the country. Fifteen thousand deaths were associated with alcohol abuse. Some researchers point out that there are far fewer users of heroin and cocaine. In 1989, it was estimated that there were five hundred thousand heroin users and four hundred deaths from heroin. Five million people used cocaine; two hundred died from the drug.

The most deadly substance was tobacco, another legal drug for adults that is illegally used by young people. Of 60 million users, tobacco caused three hundred ninety thousand deaths.[20]

Critics also argue that drugs are only partly to blame for urban problems. Years of poverty, racial prejudice, family breakdown, and government neglect have also taken a toll.

These factors may also be at least partly to blame for the problems that drug-exposed babies face. "The increasing number of children teachers are seeing who have emotional, behavioral and learning problems is probably as much a result of the increasing numbers of children who are from many generations of poverty as of drugs," said Dan R. Griffith, a psychologist at Chicago-based National Association for Perinatal Addiction Research and Education.[21]

While a pregnant woman's use of illegal drugs may affect a newborn, other substances, some legal, also take their toll. Researchers at Emory University in Atlanta found that pregnant women's use of cocaine had less effect on the behavior of their newborns than did the mothers' use of alcohol, cigarettes, or marijuana while they were pregnant.[22]

The fight against drugs is also blamed by some for contributing to the rise of crime in America.

Drug prohibition rather than drug use causes urban violence, critics say. They argue that because drugs are illegal, their sale provides tremendous profits for dealers. Drug traffickers kill to protect or seize drug turf. In Baltimore, half the murders in 1992 were drug related.[23]

If drugs were legal, these supporters argue, there would be organized ways to distribute them. Prices would be more fixed, reducing the violence. Drug sales could be taxed, bringing money to the government.

Although all communities have been affected by drugs, the inner cities have been particularly hit by drug-related violence. Critics say that government neglect of these communities has led to the conditions that make drugs and drug dealing attractive. Because many young people in these areas are unemployed, the drug trade, with its high prices, is attractive. Drug traffic may lead to turf wars.[24]

Although drugs may be a symptom as well as a cause of·social problems, a majority of Americans believe that drug use is best controlled with strict government regulations. The war on drugs carried out during the 1970s and 1980s was a response to this belief.

Let's look at the most commonly used drugs and the ways in which they are controlled.

4

Drugs of Abuse
and Their Regulation

Since the mid-1980s, penalties for drug possession and trafficking have become increasingly strict. Penalties vary from drug to drug and depend upon the amount seized and the criminal history of the offender. In many cases, a person who is guilty of a couple of relatively minor offenses can be subject to a long prison term on conviction of a third offense.

The case of Mark Young demonstrates how stiff the penalties for dealing have become.

In May of 1991, Young was arrested in his home in Indianapolis. Young had acted as a middleman, or broker, in the sale of seven hundred pounds of marijuana to buyers from Florida who were acting on the behalf of a larger buyer in New York. Although Young had never seen or handled the money or the marijuana, he was charged with conspiracy to manufacture marijuana and was held responsible for the cultivation of all the 12,500 marijuana plants grown on a nearby farm.

Young had two prior felony convictions for attempting to fill a false prescription and for the possession of a few Quaaludes and amphetamines. A felony is a more serious offense than a misdemeanor. Because of his prior convictions, he found that he could be subject to a mandatory sentence of life imprisonment without the chance of parole.[1] Although Young admittedly had committed a crime, the penalty was more severe than that received by many criminals convicted for murder.

The Controlled Substances Act

Much of the way drug offenses are treated today can be traced back to the creation of the Controlled Substance Act, also known as the CSA, created in 1970. This law combined the fifty-five existing drug laws into one uniform law. The act was strengthened with the passage of the 1986 Omnibus Drug Act. The CSA is regulated by the Department of Justice.

The CSA sets minimum guidelines that regulate the manufacture and sale of dangerous drugs. A dangerous drug has a potential for abuse and may cause harm to the user and to others. State and local governments may make the laws and penalties for drug use and sale more strict, but they must at least adhere to the minimum standards of the CSA. Most prescription drugs are not regulated by the CSA, but those that might be used by people to get high as well as for medicine are also regulated.

The Controlled Substances Act divides drugs of abuse into five schedules or categories.

Schedule I drugs are either banned or are allowed for strictly controlled experimentation. They are subject to the most severe controls, because they have a high potential for abuse as well as no currently accepted medical use in treatment in the United States.[2]

Heroin and related opiates are regulated as Schedule I drugs. So is LSD, a synthetic chemical that causes hallucinations. A hallucination is an illusion or feeling of sights and sounds that do not really exist. Other hallucinatory drugs are also regulated as Schedule I substances. It is against the law to possess or supply these drugs. Allowing a building or a residence to be used for making or supplying these drugs is also illegal.

Marijuana, a drug made from leaves and other parts of the cannabis plant, and hashish, the resin or sap scraped from the cannabis plant, are regulated as Schedule I drugs. It is illegal to possess, supply, or sell these drugs unless one has a special license. It is also illegal to grow the plant or allow one's property to be used for growing cannabis.

MDMA (3,4-methylenedioxymethamphetamine), also called Ecstasy, is another Schedule I drug.

Schedule II drugs are also highly restricted. Because cocaine can be prescribed by doctors in special circumstances, it is classified as a Schedule II drug. Other drugs in this schedule are PCP or Angel Dust (phencyclidine), some amphetamines, and some barbiturates.[3]

Drugs in schedules III, IV, and V have medical uses, but may also be misused.

Codeine is a painkiller that comes from opium. It is

similar to morphine, but weaker. Combinations of codeine and other drugs are put into schedules III and V. Morphine combinations are in Schedule III. Some barbiturates and some amphetamines are also Schedule III drugs.[4]

Schedules IV and V include prescription drugs with a lower potential for abuse. Included here are tranquilizers such as Valium® and Librium®, some mild stimulants, and sleep aids.[5]

The way a drug is used also determines whether or not it is illegal. Morphine is an opium derivative that is used to help control pain after surgery and for terminal cancer patients. Used that way, it is legal. If it is used by an addict for recreational purposes, it is illegal.[6]

The Drug Enforcement Administration

In 1973, several agencies in the Department of Justice were merged to create the Drug Enforcement Administration, the federal agency in charge of drug-law enforcement. The agency is in charge of prosecuting those who violate the controlled substances and drug-money laundering laws at the international and interstate levels of drug trafficking. In 1993, the DEA had a budget of nearly $892 million. Drug policing is a worldwide job. The DEA has offices in every state and in fifty foreign countries. It is also a dangerous job. Between 1991 and 1992, forty-five agents and employees were killed in the line of duty.[7]

The DEA enforces federal laws against the use and trafficking of illegal substances. Drug trafficking is the manufacture and distribution of illegal substances.

A DEA agent holds a brick of marijuana leaves obtained in a drug confiscation.

Let's take a look at some of these regulated illegal drugs. Why are these drugs regulated and what are the penalties for trafficking in them?

Cocaine and Crack

Cocaine is an alkaloid (a type of chemical substance) that is made from the leaf of the coca bush. When cocaine enters the body, it moves from the bloodstream to the brain and central nervous system. Users say that the drug gives them a sense of well-being, self-confidence, exhilaration, and strength. The effect lasts about fifteen to thirty minutes.

To extract the drug from the coca leaf, the leaves are mixed with sulfuric acid in a press or steel drum to make a paste called pasta or sulfata. The chemical name for this is cocaine sulfate. Hydrochloric acid is added to eliminate other chemicals. Although cocaine does have a medical use in some types of surgery, most of the drug is sold for illegal use.

Drug dealers cut or dilute the drug by adding other substances—sugar, local anesthetics, heroin, or other addictive drugs.

Usually, the drug is sniffed or snorted. Sometimes it is made into a solution, which is injected into a vein. When the drug is smoked in a specially designed water pipe, it is called freebasing.

Freebasing is especially dangerous because the ether, a substance used in the process of preparing the drug, is highly flammable. When comedian Richard Pryor tried to speed up the drying process, the ether caught fire and he was enveloped in flames, causing serious burns over his body.[8]

Crack is cocaine base that has been converted from cocaine hydrochloride. It is also referred to as "Rock." Crack cocaine, which is much cheaper than regular cocaine, is highly addictive. It was introduced into the United States in the mid-1980s, causing serious social problems.

Although occasional use of cocaine in the United States has declined since the peak year of 1985, the number of frequent abusers has not changed significantly. Among the 5 million people who used cocaine in 1992, 642,000 used it once a week or more often, compared to 662,000 in 1990.

The peak year for cocaine use by high school seniors was 1985. The good news is that fewer high school seniors in the class of 1993 used cocaine than in the class

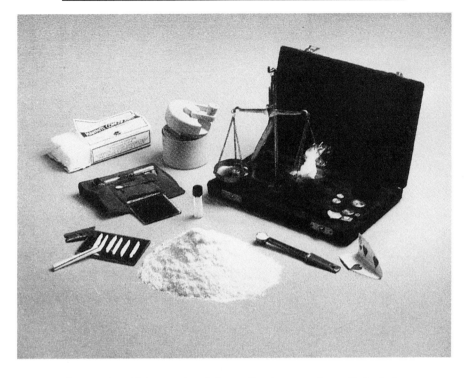

Cocaine is sold in powdered form. Cocaine paraphernalia includes razor blades, mirrors, and scales.

of 1985. The bad news is that use among tenth graders increased from 1992 to 1993.

Where Does Cocaine Come From?

Most cocaine comes from Colombia, Bolivia, and Peru. Although tons of cocaine is shipped to the United States, it appears that worldwide production has decreased slightly. In 1993, the worldwide coca leaf production was 271,700 metric tons, down from 333,900 metric tons in 1992.

Cocaine use is a serious problem in other countries,

too. Western Europe is the second largest cocaine market in the world after the United States.[9]

In 1994, the price of a gram of cocaine ranged from forty dollars to one hundred fifty dollars in the United States. Crack cocaine is sold in rocks that generally range from one tenth of a gram to half a gram. The rocks sell for as little as two dollars and as much as seventy-five dollars, but prices usually range from ten dollars to fifty dollars.[10]

Federal penalties for trafficking in cocaine and cocaine base are severe. For a first offense of possession of a 500- to 4,999-gram mixture of cocaine, a person may receive five to forty years in prison. For a second offense, the penalty is ten years to life.[11]

Heroin

In the 1990s, heroin appears to be making a comeback. Although heroin users can be found in all parts of the United States, the highest number of users can be found in the Northeast where purity of the drug is high. In 1993, the national average purity for heroin sold on the street was 35.8 percent. Ten years earlier, the purity was an average 7.0 percent. In Philadelphia, the average purity was 74.7 percent, the highest recorded for 1993.[12]

The higher purity makes the drug easier to smoke, attracting users who used to avoid the drug out of fear of using needles and getting AIDS. AIDS, the acquired immunodeficiency syndrome, is a fatal disease that is transmitted through body fluids. Addicts who reuse hypodermic needles to inject drugs into their bodies can become infected with the deadly virus.

51

Some users mix heroin and crack to make a potent and sometimes deadly drug combination called Moon Rock, Speedball, or Parachute.[13]

Louise, a twenty-nine-year-old college graduate who snorts heroin, had smoked pot and taken Ecstasy before she tried heroin. She had been afraid of using the needle to inject the drug, but when a friend showed her how to snort the drug, she decided to try it. After she uses the drug, she feels depression. "It's insidious, because when you do it, you wake up the next day and if you have any left over, you just think how you want to do it," she said. "I can see how it could worm its way into your life."[14]

In the first six months of 1991, 17,291 people were admitted to emergency rooms for heroin abuse; by 1993, the number had risen to 30,766.[15]

In 1994, a gram of heroin cost between forty dollars and five hundred dollars.[16] The penalty for trafficking less than one kilogram of heroin is not less than five years for the first offense. A second offense brings a penalty of ten years to life.[17]

Marijuana and Hashish

Marijuana and hashish come from a plant called cannabis sativa. Both are Schedule I drugs. Marijuana, made from the flowering tops and leaves of the plant, is smoked in a pipe or as a cigarette. The intoxicating ingredient in marijuana is THC, tetrahydrocannabinol. Sinsemilla, marijuana which comes from the unpollinated female plant, has a higher THC content.

It is estimated that approximately 67.5 million Americans have tried marijuana at least once in their lifetime. In 1992 alone, 17.4 million Americans used the drug at least one time. Although marijuana use has declined dramatically since 1979 when 22.5 million users were reported, recent surveys show use among high school seniors is up. In 1993, 33.3 percent of seniors questioned said they used the drug, up from 32.6 percent in 1992. Use among eighth graders is also up. In 1993, 12.6 percent of eighth graders surveyed said they had tried marijuana, up from 11.2 percent in 1992.[18]

The newest trend among these younger users is the smoking of blunts, cigars filled with marijuana and perhaps another drug.

Because many users prefer the more powerful sinsemilla marijuana, cultivation of the plant in the United States has moved indoors where a controlled environment allows the plant to be grown year-round. Marijuana also comes from Mexico, South America, and Southeast Asia.[19]

In the United States, more than 9 million arrests for marijuana-law violations have been made since 1965, with an arrest every two minutes. The majority—80 percent—of these arrests are for possession for personal use.

Penalties for marijuana possession vary from state to state. In California, a person who possesses a small amount (28.5 grams) of marijuana can be fined one hundred dollars. In Oklahoma, possession of any amount brings a possible jail sentence and five hundred dollars for the first offense. A second offense brings two to ten days in jail and a five-thousand-dollar fine. Possession of paraphernalia has a thousand-dollar fine.[20]

NORML, the National Organization for the Reform of Marijuana Laws, supports the removal of all criminal and civil penalties for the private possession of marijuana for personal use. Other organizations such as National Families in Action oppose any attempt to legalize or decriminalize the drug.

Hashish is another drug that comes from the leaves and stalks of cannabis. This drug, which is usually chewed or smoked, is not as popular in the United States as marijuana.

Most of the hashish available in the United States comes from Pakistan, Afghanistan, Lebanon, and Morocco.[21]

LSD

Lysergic acid diethylamide—LSD—was the most popular hallucinogenic drug during the 1960s. The drug took users on a trip in their own minds. Sometimes they had a pleasurable experience. Other times, the drug triggered self-destructive acts such as jumping from high places.

Although the drug is associated with the 1960s and 1970s, it is still a threat. The drug is listed as a Schedule I substance, and it is prohibited in every state. During the 1970s, use of LSD dropped.

Today, the drug is made in underground laboratories. It is sold as small tablets known as microdots, as thin squares of gelatin called windowpanes, and on sugar cubes. Blotter acid, a popular form of LSD, is sold as sheets of paper (which may have printed designs) soaked with the drug. The blotter acid form of LSD is attractive to junior high and senior high school students. The price also is attractive. The drug is inexpensive, ranging from one dollar to ten dollars per dose.

The LSD used today is less potent than that of the 1960s which is probably the reason there have been fewer LSD-related emergency-room incidents in recent years.

LSD is controlled by California-based syndicates or drug trafficking organizations. Often, the first contact with a dealer occurs at a rock concert, where an individual might meet a pusher selling a quantity up to one hundred doses. The drug is often concealed in greeting cards, cassette tapes, or articles of clothing, which are mailed to a post office box where the user can pick up the package.

LSD is not the only hallucinogen that appears on the streets. "Fantasia" is another hallucinogen that is similar in chemistry to LSD. "Nexus" is a synthetic hallucinogen that has been distributed near adult bookstores and adult theaters in Florida, Georgia, and California. Nexus produces hallucinations lasting for six to eight hours.[22]

Methamphetamine or Speed

Methamphetamine, known on the street as Crank, Speed, Go Fast, and Crystal Meth, has been called the poor man's cocaine because it is less expensive to produce than coke. The drug is a strong stimulant that gives the user a feeling of intense happiness and well-being that can last up to sixteen hours. The drug, in the form of small translucent crystals, is often smoked through a six-inch glass pipe.

The drug began as a legal stimulant, but today it is manufactured only in illegal labs. Methamphetamine labs account for more than 81 percent of all underground lab seizures, according to the DEA. Some labs are operated by outlaw motorcycle gangs and traffickers from Mexico.[23]

California is the underground methamphetamine capital of the world. Use of the drug in California skyrocketed between 1983 and 1993. Most of the users were young white males.[24]

A highly purified form of methamphetamine called Ice is a crystal form of d-methamphetamine hydrochloride. The drug gets its name because it looks like chunks of ice. Ice also goes by other names such as Quartz, Glass, Crack Meth, and Shabu.

In the summer of 1988, Ice became a popular drug in Hawaii, where it had been smuggled in from Taiwan and South Korea.

By 1990, quantities of it had spread to the mainland of the United States. The drug is manufactured in illegal labs in South Korea, Hong Kong, the Philippines, and Taiwan.

Analysis of samples of Ice seized in the United States show a high purity level—90 to 100 percent.[25]

Designer Drugs or Analogs

In the 1980s, some new drugs began to appear on the street. These were similar to controlled drugs such as heroin, but their chemical structure was slightly different. These drugs were designed specifically for abuse and to get around the scheduling law. They were made in underground laboratories. Because these substances were similar to controlled substances they were called analogs or designer drugs.

Designer drugs can be hallucinogens, narcotics, or amphetamines. PCP (phencyclidine), MDMA, fentanyl analogs, and methcathinone are four kinds of designer drugs.

PCP is known by the street names Angel Dust, Crystal, Hog, Super Grass, Killer Joints, Ozone, Wack, Embalming Fluid, and Rocket Fuel. It was developed in 1957 as a human anesthetic. An anesthetic is used in surgery to cut off the sense of pain. Because PCP had side effects of delirium and confusion, its use in human medicine was discontinued. For a few years it was used in veterinary medicine to anesthetize large primates such as apes and gorillas, but it was discontinued for that use as well. It is now classified as a Schedule II substance because it can be highly abused. Much of the available PCP is manufactured by Los Angeles-based street gangs who use buses, trains, airlines, and private cars to distribute the drug throughout the country. PCP can be sprayed on marijuana, parsley, or oregano and smoked. Sometimes, cigarettes are dipped into PCP to make Shermans or Tijuana Smalls.[26]

MDMA is known on the street as Ecstasy, XTC, Adam, E, Clarity, or Essence. MDMA is short for 3,4-methylenedioxymethamphetamine, the chemical name for the drug. MDMA has a similar chemical structure to methamphetamine or speed. Popular with middle-class youth, who use the drug at all-night dance parties called raves, MDMA or Ecstasy is fast-acting and produces sensations of alertness and emotional warmth. Users may become hyperactive. The drug may also produce the dangerous effects of disorientation and bizarre behavior. Sometimes users attempt suicide.

Fentanyl and fentanyl analogs are variations of fentanyl, a Schedule II synthetic painkiller that is a thousand times stronger than morphine. These drugs are usually sold as heroin under the different street names Tango and Cash, Goodfellas, Tombstone, Killer, Apache, Friend, and Great Bear. The drugs can be absorbed through the skin, eyes, nose, eardrums, mouth, and mucous membranes and can cause death. Between 1991 and 1992, there were at least 126 deaths related to fentanyl or fentanyl analogs in the Northeast.

Methcathinone, a synthetic stimulant sold under the street names Cat, Goob, Sniff, Stat, or Wonderstar, was first reported in 1991. It is similar in chemical formation to methamphetamine. The drug is so addictive that it was placed on Schedule I. It is distributed as a powder and is either injected or mixed with marijuana and smoked.[27]

Anabolic Steroids

Since 1991, possession of anabolic steroids, drugs that some athletes believe improve their performance and physical appearance, has been controlled by federal law. The statute placed anabolic steroids in the Schedule III class of regulated drugs.

The *Physicians' Desk Reference*, a book used by doctors to aid in writing prescriptions, states that anabolic steroids do not improve athletic ability. The drug does, however, cause serious side effects. Women users may develop unsightly acne, facial hair, thinning hair on the head, and damage to the reproductive system. Men may become sterile and may develop cancer of the testes. Other serious side effects are liver damage, increased risk of heart attack, intestinal bleeding, high blood pressure, and hypoglycemia, a lack of sugar in the blood.[28]

Although steroids are manufactured legally, the illegal market is a $300 million to $400 million industry, as of 1987.

As they are Schedule III regulated drugs, the maximum penalty for illegally dispensing or selling anabolic steroids is five years in prison and a fine of $250,000 for the first offense. For a second offense, the penalty is ten years in prison and a five hundred thousand dollar fine. The maximum penalty for simple possession of a small amount of the drug is one year in federal prison and a minimum one thousand dollar fine.

Clearly, abusing any of these drugs can be very dangerous. For more than twenty years the government has been trying to keep these substances off the street by attempting to stop them at their source and by strong law enforcement efforts.

5

The War Against Drugs

For more than twenty years the government of the United States has been waging a war on drugs. In 1971, President Nixon declared to Congress that drugs were America's Public Enemy Number One, and Congress appropriated a billion dollars to enforce drug laws and reduce drug use.

In the 1980s, presidents Ronald Reagan and George Bush revived the war on drugs. Under the Reagan administration, laws were passed that allowed federal agents to use military intelligence, training, and equipment to find and stop drug traffickers. At the state and local level, governments passed laws that allowed the police to take the assets of suspected drug dealers. Nancy Reagan, the president's wife, started the "Just Say No!" program to educate students to stay away from drugs.

In 1989, President George Bush set up the Office of National Drug Control Policy and named William Bennett as "drug czar," or leader. Under the Bush administration, billions of dollars were earmarked for the fight against drugs.

— By 1990, Bennett had declared that a victory against drugs was in sight because use of marijuana and cocaine had dropped.

Critics of the drug program disagreed. They pointed at statistics that showed that the number of daily cocaine users had gone from 246,000 in 1985 to 336,000 in 1990. Hard-core addiction, they said, was not under control. Some Americans will always use drugs, they said. In spite of the money spent to fight the drug problems, they claimed, drugs are as widespread as they were before the government began the war on drugs.[1]

Turf wars and drive-by shootings, which often claimed innocent victims, continued.

The Crime Control Act of 1994 provided for the addition of a hundred thousand officers to the nation's police force and added prison space for violent drug offenders. The 1996 presidential request for fighting drugs, $14.6 billion, is the largest in history.[2]

To better understand the government's role in fighting illegal substances, it is necessary to look at the business of drugs.

The Business of Drugs

Drugs are a big business. Although many Americans disagree about how to treat individual drug users, most support the government's efforts to fight drug dealers and traffickers, whom they consider to be responsible for the drug problem. Drug dealing is both national and international in scope. Drugs such as amphetamine and methamphetamine are mostly made in underground laboratories located in the United States. Heroin and cocaine originate mostly in foreign countries.

Many people are involved in the distribution of drugs, especially those that come from a foreign country. The manufacturer may be part of a drug cartel. A cartel is a partnership or syndicate that attempts to corner the market in coca or opium. The economies of some under-developed countries may be tied to the production of drugs. Many peasants earn their livelihood from tending drug crops.

Drug importers work with smugglers to introduce the drug into other countries for distribution. Smugglers are involved with transporting the drug. There are many ways to do this—by airplane, boat, car, truck, or trailer, or by hiding drugs on a person's body. After a drug comes into the country, traffickers spread the drug to other areas.

Distributors deal in large quantities of drugs and may hide behind a legitimate business front. Dealers are usually people who sell many ounces of a product. A dealer-user is a small-time distributor who sells drugs to help support his or her own habit.

Drug dealers will attempt to use others to help transport drugs. These people are called mules. A mule might be a woman who straps a kilogram of cocaine to her stomach area so that she looks pregnant. Or a mule might be a college student who has small packets of heroin taped to his arms and legs, hidden under clothing.[3]

It is easier to arrest those who are at a lower level in the drug distribution chain. Arresting and prosecuting those at the top is more difficult.

Interdiction

Because much of the illicit drugs come from other countries, the fight against drugs is international in scope. Stopping drug trafficking and seizing drugs at international borders is called interdiction. United States customs agents check the personal belongings of people entering the country to see if they might be smuggling drugs. They also check shipments of goods that come across international borders. The United States Coast Guard patrols the coastlines to keep smugglers from bringing drugs into the country by sea.

Interdiction is difficult because the United States has more than five thousand miles of borders with Canada and almost two thousand miles with Mexico. Much of the border area is wilderness or desert. Add to that the many miles of coastline over which drugs may pass and airspace over which drug-laden planes can fly, and you can see how hard it is to keep drug smugglers out of the country.

Drug traffickers try many roundabout ways to smuggle drugs into the United States. Some Colombian drug smugglers have used submarinelike ships to sneak cocaine to Puerto Rico for shipment to the United States. Because the ships ride low in the water, they are very difficult to see on the open sea. The traffickers also use more conventional methods of smuggling such as hiding drugs in fishing boats that sail along the coast of Mexico and Central America. Drugs are also hidden in baggage and cargo on airliners.[4]

In spite of the difficulty, the number of international drug seizures reported by the U.S. State Department has increased since 1989. In 1993, 41 metric tons of opium,

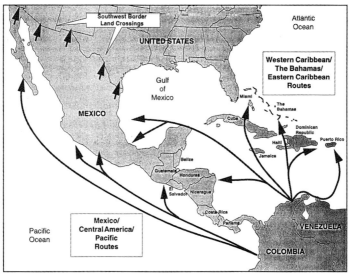

Primary Noncommercial Air/Maritime Cocaine Trafficking Routes

265 metric tons of cocaine, and 2,886 metric tons of marijuana and hashish were seized.

Unfortunately, these drugs still are available in large enough quantities to satisfy demand at a relatively low price and high purity. This does not mean that the law enforcement efforts have not worked. Without their efforts, there would probably be even more drugs in the country.[5]

Interdiction also involves fighting drugs at their source—in the foreign countries where they originate.

Peru, for example, is thought to be the source of more than 60 percent of the world's supply of coca.[6] Bolivia and Colombia also are major suppliers of cocaine. Much of the coca grown and pounded into paste in Bolivia and Peru is then sent to Colombia to be processed into cocaine. To stem the tide of cocaine, the United

States has tried to persuade these countries to work to eliminate coca. The United States would like to encourage these countries to disrupt the cocaine-trafficking organizations or cartels by destroying crops, arresting drug lords, and prosecuting them to send them to prison.[7]

Some critics question whether it is appropriate for the United States to get involved in the politics and problems of foreign countries. They say that anti-narcotics programs abroad may help support dictatorial governments. In June 1990, Congress began investigations to find out if the Bush administration's plan to spend approximately $40 million to train the Peruvian military to fight drug traffickers was really a way to help fight leftist rebels there.

"It is a backdoor slide into military involvement in another country," said Congressman John F. Kerry, chairman of the Senate Subcommittee on Narcotics, Terrorism, and International Operations.[8]

Coca has become a profitable crop for the countries where it is grown, more profitable than other enterprises such as growing coffee or raising livestock. It is difficult to convince poor farmers to stop growing the plant. Governments in these countries may agree in theory with the United States when it comes to eliminating drug crops, but they sometimes have trouble developing a concrete plan of action. Even the projected millions of dollars in United States aid does not pay for the loss of a crop that is worth four times that amount.

Critics argue that the millions of dollars spent to stop drug production at the source is not effective.

In 1994, the Colombian Supreme Court made legal the use and possession of small amounts of some drugs.

The government has not arrested and prosecuted drug cartel leaders. Safety of witnesses and their families is not guaranteed in drug cases.

In Bolivia, government destruction of coca crops is at a standstill, and government corruption is rampant. Peru remains the largest supplier of cocaine in the world.

In Mexico, which supplies opium and marijuana, efforts in 1994 resulted in more seizures, but opium production is up. Cocaine still passes through Mexico on the way to the United States.[9]

Critics also argue that American efforts are random, focusing more attention on the countries that produce coca than on areas that grow other drug crops such as the opium poppy. For example, the United States has not tried to make Pakistan stop its $5-billion-a-year heroin industry, which provides one third of the drug for America's estimated 500,000 to 1,000,000 heroin addicts.[10]

Eradication

Eradication is a term the DEA uses to describe the removal and destruction of drug crops. In the United States, marijuana is the crop that is most often targeted for removal. When agents find marijuana fields, they may spray them with an herbicide to kill the plants.

Marijuana is the most commonly used illegal drug in the United States. Surveys indicate that the drug is growing in popularity with high school seniors and younger students. The Drug Abuse Warning Network (DAWN) shows that the number of accident victims who test positive for marijuana is also up.

Twenty to twenty-five percent of all marijuana is grown in the United States. In 1993, the five major states for total plants eradicated were South Dakota, Indiana, Missouri, Illinois, and Wisconsin.

Because marijuana growing is a business with big profits, growers try to hide their crops from federal agents.

They want to avoid arrests and harsh mandatory minimum sentences. Many have begun to move their operations indoors into greenhouses. The top five states for indoor cultivation of marijuana were California, Washington, Oregon, Florida, and Wisconsin. The average indoor crop has approximately eighty-seven plants so that growers, if caught, will avoid prosecution under the mandatory sentence for one hundred or more plants. To avoid arrest, growers sometimes set booby traps to keep agents away from their plants. Some bury land mines, which blow up when the agents step on them.[11]

Some critics argue that the eradication program unfairly targets marijuana. Legal substances such as

DEA agents seek out marijuana crops in order to destroy them. Some marijuana is grown indoors in greenhouses to avoid detection.

tobacco kill far more people than does marijuana, yet federal subsidies, or grants of money, help tobacco farmers make a profit from their crops.

On the other hand, opponents to legalization of marijuana point out that tobacco kills more people because more people have access to it. Making another harmful substance legal just does not make sense, they argue.

Money Laundering

Because dealing drugs is illegal, much of the business is done in cash. Some drug dealers have a flashy lifestyle, but spending too much money in cash is also dangerous.

Trying to hide drug money in a legitimate business enterprise is called money laundering. Because drug dealers cheat the government out of income tax, the Internal Revenue Service (IRS) has set up safeguards against money laundering. In the United States, any bank that receives a deposit of over ten thousand dollars is required to report the deposit to the IRS.

Because retail businesses that collect large amounts of cash are exempt from the ten thousand dollar rule, drug dealers have been known to create or buy existing companies through which to channel their profits.

To avoid being caught, some drug dealers put their money into foreign banks that allow secret bank accounts.

It is believed that drug barons launder as much as $100 billion a year from profits they make in the United States.[12]

Mandatory Minimum Sentences

When Nicole Richardson was in high school, she fell in love with Jeff, a small-time drug dealer. She was arrested and charged with drug dealing because she told an informant who was trying to buy LSD where to find Jeff. Jeff cooperated with the prosecutor to help make other drug busts and was given a reduced sentence of five years. Because Nicole had not used or sold drugs, she said she was innocent. Her case went to trial. She was found guilty of drug trafficking, an offense that carried a mandatory minimum sentence of ten years in prison without parole. Although the judge called it a total miscarriage of justice, he was required to carry out the sentence.[13]

Mandatory minimum sentences are sentencing guidelines that went into effect in 1987 after Congress had passed the Sentencing Reform Act of 1984. The act was a reaction to the growing drug problem of the 1980s. Although mandatory minimum sentences had existed in the 1950s, they had been repealed in the late 1960s because they were considered a failure. After repeal, judges were able to consider many factors when

Drug Enforcement Agency officers inspect marijuana plants found during a drug seizure. These plants will be destroyed.

sentencing a criminal to prison. Was he a first time offender? How serious was her involvement? Today, where drugs are concerned, judges are not allowed to look at any factors in sentencing except for the drug and its weight.[14]

A criticism of mandatory minimum sentences is that the person who is most to blame may receive the shortest sentence because he or she can trade information about friends who may have less involvement. Those who have done the least have less information to use in a plea bargain. Like Nicole, such people may receive the longest prison sentences. According to findings by the U.S. Sentencing Commission, low-level drug participants receive mandatory minimum sentences 70 percent of the time while top-level traffickers receive them only 60 percent of the time.

Families Against Mandatory Minimums (FAMM) is an organization that was founded by Julie Stewart in 1991 after her brother was arrested as the head of a marijuana conspiracy and received a five-year mandatory minimum sentence. Julie believed that he had been framed.

FAMM believes that the mandatory minimum sentencing law is unjust. Blacks and Hispanics receive mandatory minimum sentences more often than do whites arrested for similar crimes. According to statistics of the U.S. Sentencing Commission, 88.3 percent of federal crack cocaine offenders in 1993 were black, even though 65 percent of the people who have used crack cocaine in their lifetime are white. A high number of those crack defendants sentenced to prison are often street-level dealers. Only a small number of those in prison were high-level dealers.[15]

6

Search and Seizure— Testing Fourth Amendment Rights

The right of the people to be secure in their persons, houses, papers, and effects, against unreasonable searches and seizures, shall not be violated, and no warrants shall issue, but upon probable cause, supported by oath or affirmation and particularly describing the place to be searched, and the persons or things to be seized.

—The Fourth Amendment

To win a war, it is sometimes necessary to use exceptional means to fight the enemy. In the process, individual rights can be threatened. Critics claim that vigorous efforts to combat drugs can violate constitutional rights.

Senator Edward M. Kennedy wrote, "Our constitutional rights do not contribute to the drug problem, and compromising them will not solve it. We do not need to trample the Bill of Rights to win the war on drugs."[1]

The Fourth Amendment to the Constitution protects individuals from unreasonable search or seizure of property. This means that there must be a reasonable suspicion of wrongdoing.

It is true that people do go to great lengths to hide drugs and drug use. To catch the few who use drugs at work or at school, does the government, an employer, or a school district have the right to force individuals, even those not suspected of drug use, to submit to urine tests to determine drug use? Should the police be able to search a suspect without a warrant just because the

People have gone to great lengths to hide drugs. In the 1920s and 1930s, people would sometimes hide drugs in the heels of their shoes.

At this school in Newport Beach, California, a sign warns of the dangers of selling or possessing drugs on or near the school grounds.

person may look like someone who uses drugs? Should the government be allowed to seize property in instances that may involve drugs? These are serious questions that involve the rights of the individual as protected by the United States Constitution.

Students are involved in these questions as more and more schools attempt to fight delinquency and drug abuse through mandatory urine tests and locker searches. All young people, even those who have never taken drugs, are affected.

In 1991, twelve-year-old James Acton, a good student who had never used drugs, found out that he would have to pass a mandatory drug test by urinalysis in order to play on the football team.

The Oregon school district where James's school was located was concerned about a growing drug problem. In 1989, a drug-testing program was started. School officials believed that some student athletes had been smoking marijuana and using other drugs.

When James's parents refused to sign the consent form for drug testing, he was suspended from athletics. His parents decided to take the school district to court, stating that the tests violated James's constitutional rights protected under the Fourth Amendment. The case was heard at several different levels in the justice system. Finally, in 1994, the United States Supreme Court ruled that routine drug testing of school athletes was constitutional and did not violate Fourth Amendment rights.[2]

Mandatory Drug Tests, Pros and Cons

Opponents to mandatory drug testing at school and in the workplace believe that the tests invade individual privacy. Urinalysis, they say, is a form of body search. To avoid cheating, an employee may be required to urinate in front of a witness. Opponents object to tests that target all workers or students, not just those who are suspected of substance abuse.

The American Civil Liberties Union (ACLU) is an organization that protects an individual's constitutional rights. Members of the ACLU oppose indiscriminate urine testing because they believe the process is unfair and unnecessary. They say that it is unfair because workers and students who are not suspected of using drugs are still forced to prove their innocence through an embarrassing test. It is unnecessary because the tests cannot predict whether a worker can perform his or her job or whether a student is a danger to others.

The ACLU claims that the urine tests can be unreliable. According to the ACLU, laboratory error can confuse similar chemical compounds. Codeine and cough syrup have sometimes produced positive results for heroin. A student who has taken ibuprofen might test positive for marijuana. A worker who has taken Nyquil might test positive for amphetamines.

Even if the tests are accurate, they cannot tell when the drug was used. An employee who smoked marijuana on Saturday night may test positive on Wednesday even though the effects of the drug have worn off. At the other extreme, an employee who snorts cocaine on the way to work may have a negative urine test because the drug has not yet been absorbed into the person's system.[3]

On the other hand, companies who conduct random drug tests in the workplace believe that drugs have a serious effect on workplace safety, performance, and morale. They point to a tragic example of workplace drug abuse as an example.

On January 4, 1987, in Chase, Maryland, 16 people were killed, 170 were injured, and damages were estimated at $100 million when Amtrack and Conrail trains collided. The engineer who was responsible for the accident had driven his engine through three warning lights onto the main high-speed corridor between Washington, D.C., and New York City. He admitted to having smoked marijuana just before the accident. His drug use was discovered through mandatory drug testing after the accident.[4]

How serious a problem are drugs in the workplace? Of the employed cocaine users who called the National Cocaine Hotline (l-800-COCAINE) in 1989, 74 percent said they used drugs at work. Of these, 83 percent used cocaine while working. Other drugs were also used on the job: 39 percent used alcohol, and 33 percent used marijuana. Sixty-four percent said drugs are easy to obtain at work, and 44 percent said they sold drugs at work. Eighteen percent reported having stolen money from coworkers and 20 percent said they had been involved in a drug-related accident at work.[5]

More recent statistics, however, show a drop in workplace drug use. In 1994, according to SmithKline Beecham Clinical Labs, 7.5 percent of 3.6 million workers tested positive for drugs, down from 8.4 percent in 1993. The rate has declined for the past seven years.[6]

Those who defend mandatory drug tests believe students and employees will think twice before using drugs if they have to pass drug tests. Those who are using drugs occasionally may even be helped if their use is caught before they become addicted.[7]

Do Drug Tests Work?

One study of 4,964 applicants for jobs with the United States Postal Service in Boston indicated that there is a relationship between cocaine or marijuana use and poor performance on the job.

The researchers asked the applicants to provide a urine sample, which would be tested for cocaine and

Stores such as The Home Depot warn applicants that they will be tested for illegal drug use before being hired.

marijuana. They then tracked the records of those applicants who were hired. Of the 2,537 applicants who were hired, 198 tested positive for marijuana and 55 tested positive for cocaine. While the nondrug users had an absentee rate of only 4 percent, the marijuana users were found to have an absentee rate of 7.1 percent. The cocaine users were absent at a 9.8 percent rate.

The drug users also had more accidents. Workers who had marijuana in their urine samples had 55 percent more accidents and 85 percent more injuries. People who tested positive for cocaine had an 85 percent increase in injuries.[8]

Those who support random drug tests say that an estimated $100 billion is lost each year because of drug-related absenteeism, health-care costs, and high accident rates. About 50 percent of Fortune 500 corporations require tests. Drug-test supporters believe that airline pilots and transportation workers also should be required to pass urine tests.[9]

Are School Drug Tests Justified?

Most people seem to agree that drug use at school is a serious problem. According to the "School Crime" survey report, nearly one third of the students questioned said marijuana was easily obtained. Eleven percent said cocaine was easy to get; 9 percent said crack was also easy to buy.[10]

Statistics from 1994, collected by the National Institute on Drug Abuse (NIDA), confirm that drug use is up on school campuses. Still, only a minority of students are using drugs. Lifetime drug use among all eighth graders showed that 16.7 percent had used marijuana; 19.9, inhalants; 4.3, hallucinogens; 3.7, LSD; 3.6, cocaine; and 2.4, crack cocaine. In 1991, lifetime use by eighth graders was slightly lower. Among those students, 10.2 percent had used marijuana; 17.6, inhalants; 3.2, hallucinogens; 2.7, LSD; 2.3, cocaine; and 1.3, crack cocaine.[11]

In the Vernonia, Oregon, school district where James Acton went to school, there was disagreement as to whether mandatory urine tests of student athletes were justified. The school district argued that when students choose to go out for athletics, they should be fit to participate in the sport. They argued that drug use harms a player's physical fitness and may endanger others. Those opposed to the urine tests argued that the district was inflating the drug problem because only three students had failed the urine test in four years.[12]

In 1995, the case was heard by the United States Supreme Court. A majority of the justices voted that random drug tests of high school athletes did not violate their constitutional rights.

Justice Antonin Scalia said, "Students are kids. You're dealing with children. You're not dealing with adults." Thomas Christ, an attorney for the American Civil Liberties Union Foundation of Oregon disagreed. He said that forcing a student to take a urine test is "an intrusive, degrading experience."[13]

Drug Testing and Athletics

Drug use by athletes poses a special problem. It has been estimated that as many as 11 percent of high school athletes are using steroids to develop muscles and build body strength. The side effects include liver damage, psychotic aggressiveness, increased acne, reproductive problems, cardiovascular (heart) damage, and body hair growth on girls.

"Steroids are easier to get than most illegal drugs because people are not paying attention," said Keith Lee of Northeastern University Center for the Study of Sport and Society.[14]

In professional sports, drug testing has been controversial. The most demanding tests are carried out at the Olympic Games. Olympic officials began drug testing in 1967 when they were looking for drugs such as amphetamines that might give an athlete an edge to win. Anabolic steroids were added to their list of banned substances in 1973. At the Los Angeles Olympics in 1984, the first, second, and third-place winners were required to give two samples of urine after their event. The first sample was stored away in tight security. The second was sent to a laboratory maintained by the International Olympic Committee. If the result was positive for drugs, the athlete and his or her team officials were told. A second urinalysis was tested. If that also came up positive, the athlete was stripped of his or her medal.[15]

Drugs in the Military

In the 1980s, the American military had a serious drug problem. Soldiers, sailors, and marines were reporting for duty red-eyed, wobbly, and nauseated. Many had to be sent home or hospitalized.

In a study commissioned by the Defense Department, it was revealed that one in four people in uniform was using some kind of illegal substance. The rates of abuse were 29 percent of the army, 33 percent of the navy, 37 percent of the marine corps, and 14 percent of the air force.

The military decided to adopt a tough policy to reduce drug use, beginning with random drug testing. Personnel at all levels of the military never knew when they would be tested. Drug users were given treatment, counseling, and rehabilitation. As a result, drug use dropped dramatically. By 1992, only 5.8 percent or one in seventeen members of the Armed Forces was abusing drugs. Today, a recruit must test negative for drugs before being sworn in. There are approximately 3 million drug tests annually.[16]

Does Property Seizure Violate Constitutional Rights?

Under the Fourth Amendment, citizens are also protected against unreasonable seizure of their property and assets.

Sam Zhadanov has been serving a five-year sentence for money laundering, conspiracy to sell drug paraphernalia, and conspiracy to help in the distribution of crack cocaine.

Zhadanov, a sixty-eight-year-old Russian immigrant, was owner of a plastic molding business. His problems began when two customers asked him to make small plastic containers which they said were for perfume. The bottles were labeled "For Perfume Sample Use Only." Because the customers were often late in their payments, Zhadanov sometimes took payment in cash as well as by check.

It turned out that the customers were using the bottles to hold crack cocaine. Because crack is illegal, the containers that carry it and the money used to make them are also illegal. The company that accepts the money is considered guilty of drug trafficking and money laundering.

Zhadanov was charged with conspiracy to distribute ten thousand kilograms of crack and with sixty-nine money laundering counts, based on checks he had received for the bottles. The government did not say that he had ever seen or sold crack cocaine.

At first Zhadanov was determined to fight the charges because he believed he was innocent, but his attorney urged him to sign a plea agreement to avoid a long prison term. Zhadanov was also afraid that the government might make charges against his wife, a co-owner of the business.

The government seized the Zhadanovs' personal bank accounts, the company bank account, the factory, the equipment, and the land on which it was located.[17]

Fighting drug trafficking and drug abuse is a serious and dangerous effort in America's drug policy, but how far should the government go in the efforts to reduce drugs? How important are the rights of the individual?

"Our Fourth Amendment is so important that it must be protected no matter what," James Acton said.[18]

What do you think about this issue?

7

The Case for Legalization

Federal, state, and local governments have been successful in breaking up drug rings, uncovering money laundering schemes, arresting and jailing dealers and users, and confiscating and destroying tons of cocaine, marijuana, and heroin. In spite of this, the drug problem still exists.

Spending vast amounts of money to combat drugs has been a failure, say critics. In late 1991, the General Accounting Office, the government agency that oversees the way the federal government spends money, reported that the Pentagon's interdiction efforts had not affected the flow of drugs into the country. These efforts had cost close to one billion dollars. With so much money being spent, why is there still a serious drug problem?

The vast amounts of money that can be made from drug trafficking means that dealers will always look for a way to supply users, regardless of the risk. Drug lords consider the efforts to stop drugs as a nuisance rather than a real threat. For every ten kilos (kilograms) of cocaine distributed in the United States, one or two are seized by law enforcement.

Some experts believe that destruction of crops at the source is also useless. In 1992, the governments of Peru, Bolivia, and Colombia destroyed hundreds of cocaine-production sites, but neither the total cocaine production nor the ease of buying the drug in the United States was affected.[1]

Since the cost of creating most illegal drugs is not much different from the cost of producing coffee, alcohol, and tobacco, the high price that users must pay makes huge profits for organized crime. In 1986, marijuana and heroin each created $7 billion in profits, and cocaine produced over $13 billion. If these products were legal, the government could collect billions of dollars in taxes, money that now goes to support organized crime, say critics of the current drug policy.[2]

Problems of Prohibition

Government efforts to fight drugs are sometimes compared to the years of Prohibition (1919–1933) when alcoholic beverages were illegal. Prohibition was a dismal failure. Violence was commonplace in some cities as alcohol-trafficking mobs fought one another for control of turf. Law enforcement efforts were directed toward finding and destroying illegal liquor and arresting bootleggers. A bootlegger was a person who made or sold liquor illegally. In spite of the efforts, alcoholic beverages were still available, and were more dangerous than before because there were no standards for producing liquor. Some liquor was as strong as 190 proof—nearly pure alcohol.

84

Prohibition of alcohol under the Eighteenth Amendment created violence as criminal gangs fought each other over turf. Here, police chase a suspected bootlegger.

Drug prohibition creates similar problems. The current policy creates six side effects, says David Boaz, vice president of the Cato Institute, a research organization that explores drug issues.

First, crime has increased because drugs are illegal, Boaz and other experts say. Because drugs are illegal, dealers cannot go to court to solve their disputes. Instead, they turn to violence such as drive-by shootings. Because drugs are very expensive, users may commit crimes to pay for them. Desperate addicts will become prostitutes, rob, steal, or kill to get money to support their habits.

Second, illegal drugs also cause corruption. In some cities renegade police officers cooperate with crack dealers.

The case of Fonda Cecilia Moore, a policewoman in the District of Colombia, is an example. On the side, Fonda, a model officer, moonlighted as a partner of one of the biggest cocaine dealers in Washington, D.C. She has been charged with conspiring to commit murder and to distribute crack cocaine.[3] In another case in New York City, a group of eight police officers faked calls to a 911 emergency number to give themselves an excuse for breaking into drug dealers' apartments to steal money and drugs.[4]

Third, drugs also bring users into contact with criminals. This is especially dangerous for young users because they are sometimes recruited to work for drug pushers.

A fourth effect is the creation of stronger drugs such as crack. If a drug trafficker can smuggle only one suitcase of drugs into the country or drive only one car filled with drugs into a city, he or she will choose the more profitable drug. During Prohibition, bootleggers would produce stronger liquor, and the production of beer went down. Crack was unknown until the 1980s, a decade when strict laws against drug use were in effect.

Fifth, drug prohibition also contributes to the spread of HIV virus, which causes AIDS, through contaminated, dirty hypodermic needles. Addicts share needles in areas where possessing them is illegal. Intravenous drug use is the single largest source of new HIV infection.[5]

A sixth effect of prohibition is the erosion of civil liberties. Critics believe that some drug urine tests, seizure of personal property, and lengthy prison sentences violate the constitutional amendments protecting citizens against unreasonable search and seizure and unfair imprisonment.[6]

Critics point out that minorities are targeted for prosecution and stiffer penalties for drugs more often than are whites in spite of the fact that federal surveys show that 69 percent of all cocaine users are white.[7]

In California, white crack offenders are more often prosecuted in state courts where sentences are far less. Minorities are more likely to be tried in federal courts, which enforce mandatory minimum sentences. The difference in penalties can be up to eight years for the same offense.[8]

Drug Decriminalization and Legalization

Many people argue that the drug problem should be approached in other ways. Some say that drug addiction is a disease that should be treated as a public health concern rather than a criminal justice issue. They argue that hard-core addicts should be given treatment on demand. These advocates believe that users should be given enough drugs to maintain their habits as a way to take the profit out of drugs. This might keep drug users from criminal activities such as burglary and robbery to get money for drugs.

Decriminalization means that while selling drugs would still be against the law, possession of a quantity for personal use would not be illegal for adults. Full legalization means that no drug possession would be against the law for adults. In some cases, drugs might even be legally sold to adults in much the same way that tobacco and alcohol are sold today. It is likely that drug use by minors would still be against the law.

Those who argue for legalization or decriminalization

87

of drugs do not agree on details. Would all drugs be legal? Would addicts have to register in order to buy legal drugs? Would drugs be advertised such as cigarettes and alcohol are currently promoted? Would drugs be sold in government-operated stores, at convenience stores, at the supermarket? Would drug users be licensed? Would they be taxed? How would drugs be regulated in regard to purity and potency? How would reformers go about changing the drug laws? Would the law differ from state to state?

Let's look at some of the ways drugs could be decriminalized or in some cases, legalized. First, laws would have to be changed to take away the illegal status of drugs.

Changing the Law

There are several ways to change laws in the United States—repeal, decriminalization, de facto legalization, and outright legalization. These changes can be accomplished by popular vote, court decision, or by a bill enacted by a legislature at the state or federal level.

Because the Supreme Court has upheld random drug tests and searches for drugs without warrants, it is not likely that it would rule in favor of legalization.

Another way to change the law would be for citizens to gather signatures on petitions. If they can obtain enough signatures supporting their cause, the proposal, called an initiative, is placed on the ballot. Voters then decide if they want to make this initiative a part of the law. Because public opinion is not strongly in favor of drug legalization, it is not likely that such an initiative would win. This was the case in 1986 when the Oregon

Marijuana Initiative was able to collect enough signatures to put a proposal to legalize marijuana on the ballot. Only 27 percent of the voters voted for the proposal.[9]

Another way to change the law is to bring the issue before the legislature at the state or federal level. Legislatures could pass laws making certain drugs legal. For example, Congress could repeal the Harrison Act of 1914, which opened the door to prosecuting drug users.

It would also be possible to leave the laws in place, but simply not enforce them. This is called de facto legalization. Decriminalization of drugs would allow for enforcement of the laws against drugs, but would permit a court to give an offender a lesser punishment such as a citation and fine rather than a prison sentence. Receiving a citation is similar to being given a ticket for a traffic violation.

In the case of marijuana, this form of decriminalization exists in eleven states—Alaska, California, Colorado, Maine, Minnesota, Mississippi, Nebraska, New York, North Carolina, Ohio, and Oregon. In these states, if a person is caught with a small amount of the drug, he or she would get a citation and a fine. The amount varies from state to state.

In other states, however, stiff penalties still exist for possession of even a small amount of marijuana. In Nevada, use or possession of one to six ounces carries a five thousand dollar fine for the first offense. In Kansas, possession of any amount of marijuana or drug paraphernalia carries a twenty-five hundred dollar fine.[10]

Kurt Schmoke, mayor of Baltimore, has argued in favor of decriminalizing some drugs in order to pull addicts into the public health system. Criminal penalties for drug possession would be removed, and health professionals would be allowed to prescribe a dose of a currently illegal drug to help treat an addict. Drugs would not be given to nonusers. Allowing addicts to exchange their dirty needles for clean ones is a form of decriminalization.[11]

How Would Legalization Work?

Let's look at some of the proposals for drug legalization. Some supporters believe that drugs should be regulated by the states rather than by federal laws. Ethan Nadelmann, a supporter of drug legalization, argues for allowing more local control of the drug problem. He believes that the federal government, which schedules illegal substances, should allow towns, cities, counties, and states to experiment with solutions that fit their particular situations. As an example, he points to the repeal of Prohibition, which involved local option. This allowed some states to legalize wine and beer and others to remain dry. Some states had monopolies where all liquor was sold at state stores. Others allowed liquor to be sold at markets.[12]

Nadelmann argues for decriminalization for possession and sale of small amounts of marijuana by adults. He also advocates making it a prescription drug for sufferers of cancer, AIDS, multiple sclerosis, and other illnesses that might be helped by its use.

He also has suggestions for the regulation of some hard drugs. Heroin use could be reduced by getting addicts to switch to methadone, a substitute for the drug. Methadone, he argues, helps addicts to cut down on heroin use, eliminates criminal activities to finance drugs, and helps reduce exposure to diseases such as AIDS that are passed through dirty needles. He says that a heroin addict who wants methadone should be treated like a person with diabetes who needs insulin to stay alive. He advocates allowing physicians to write methadone prescriptions that could be filled at a local pharmacy. In some cities, such as Boston and Baltimore, methadone is dispensed from mobile vans. To keep addicts in the health system, even those who have a relapse and return to illegal drug use are still able to stay in the methadone program.

Nadelmann believes that a good drug policy should have three parts. First, it would be legal to possess a small quantity of any drug for personal use. Second, adults could legally obtain drugs that had a certified quality, purity, and quantity. Third, citizens would have the power to make their own decisions about drugs and whether or not to use them.[13]

NORML and the Decriminalization of Marijuana

NORML (National Organization for the Reform of Marijuana Laws) was founded in 1970 by Keith Stoup, an activist. The purpose of the organization is to end all penalties for adults who want to use, cultivate, or possess marijuana. The organization tries to educate the public about marijuana and marijuana laws and to legalize the drug.[14]

NORML supports reasonable regulation of large-scale cultivation and sale of the drug and of driving under the influence. Although the organization does not promote the use of marijuana or any other drug, they believe that the current laws are unjust and that millions of Americans have already decided to break the law by smoking pot.[15]

Advocates of legalization of marijuana do not believe that smoking pot leads to more serious drugs. They point to the Netherlands where only 13.6 percent of twelve- to eighteen-year-olds smoke pot in spite of its easy availability. Only about 0.3 percent of the same age group is reported to have used cocaine during the past thirty days. On the other hand, in the United States, where marijuana is illegal, there has been an increase in pot use with 38 percent of high school seniors reporting that they have tried the drug. During the 1980s, as marijuana use declined, cocaine use increased.[16]

Through the years NORML has filed lawsuits to change marijuana laws. One suit fought government spraying of paraquat, a poisonous herbicide, on illegal marijuana crops.

Another successfully led to the development of a synthetic THC (the intoxicating substance in marijuana) pill for legal use by cancer patients to help fight the side effects of chemotherapy.[17]

Use of Illegal Drugs in Medicine

Bob Randall, a one-time Washington, D.C., cab driver, is one of eight people in the United States who can legally smoke marijuana. Randall suffers from glaucoma, a disease that increases the pressure inside the eye. If not treated, the sufferer will go blind.

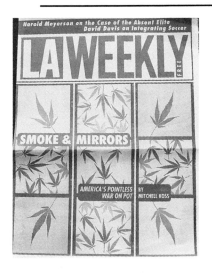

Some alternative newspapers such as *LA Weekly* question the government's war against marijuana.

When Randall discovered that smoking marijuana reduced the pressure in his eye, he started smoking every day. In 1975, he was arrested for marijuana possession. He was acquitted when the court decided that he had the right to save his eyesight, even if it meant breaking the law.

Today, the government provides him with marijuana through the Compassionate Use Investigational New Drug program, because the Federal Drug Administration is gathering data on the effects of the drug.

Federal health authorities insist that Marinol, a synthetic drug that contains THC, the main ingredient in marijuana, gives the same relief, but patients who have tried both claim that it does not.

The Cannabis Buyers' Club, an underground pharmacy in San Francisco, is part of a growing movement to help sick people obtain marijuana for medicinal use. Across the country, thousands of patients who have AIDS, cancer, glaucoma, epilepsy, multiple sclerosis, and other illnesses defy the law to buy marijuana to help relieve their pain and symptoms.[18]

Tacoma attorney Ralph Seeley believes that marijuana has provided the best relief for the side effects of his bone and lung cancer treatment. The treatment, chemotherapy, which is used to try to stop the growth of cancer cells, caused him to have severe nausea. Cancer patients, he says, are often unable to take Marinol. Because of their nausea, they throw up the pill.[19]

Researchers believe that LSD and other mind-altering psychedelic drugs could help people who suffer from mental illness and might even help drug addiction. In the early 1970s, the federal government banned psychedelic drug research on human subjects. In the 1990s, a few researchers have permission to look into these substances for possible medical benefits.

Some researchers say that psychedelic drugs can open the mind to psychotherapy, bringing forth repressed memories. The researchers believe that these drugs might also help people work on attempts to end dependence on drugs.[20]

Heroin is another drug that is a powerful painkiller. While some cancer patients can be treated with morphine and other legal painkillers, others cannot. Heroin is twice as potent as morphine. It acts faster and is less painful as an injection because it can be dissolved easily in liquid. In Great Britain it is legal to use heroin in hospices to help cancer patients deal with extreme pain. A hospice is a group home for patients who are close to dying. It is illegal to use heroin in this way in the United States. Opponents say that there are better drugs to treat pain. They also fear that the medical supply of heroin might be stolen from hospitals for resale on the street. Still, the questions remains: Should a cancer patient who cannot be helped with other drugs be allowed to take heroin to help relieve the pain?[21]

Many Dangerous Substances Are Legal

Advocates for legalization point out that while some dangerous substances are targeted for prohibition, others remain legal and readily available.

Fifteen-year-old Jennifer Jones of Palm Beach Gardens, Florida, was aware of the danger of drugs like crack cocaine and heroin. She did not know that Freon drained from an air conditioner was also dangerous. Police think that a friend showed her how to sniff the drug from a plastic bag, which caused her to become unconscious. She was unable to remove the plastic bag from her face, and she continued to breathe Freon until she died.

More than a thousand people nationwide die from sniffing or "huffing" toxic substances each year. Inhalants rank as the third-most-used drug, after alcohol and marijuana, in the United States. National surveys have found that 20 percent of all eighth graders have huffed toxic substances. "It's becoming more mainstream. Kids say, 'I can get this. It's cheap and easy to get, and I'm not going to get busted for it,'" said Harvey Weiss, chairman of the National Inhalant Prevention Coalition in Austin, Texas.

If legally obtained inhalants are the third-ranked drug for teens, then why should other drugs, less used, continue to be scheduled as illegal, critics ask.[22]

Herbs available in health food stores are also largely unregulated. These substances can be used to improve mood and sexual performance, and to increase energy.

In Texas, authorities believe that *ma huang,* an herbal diet supplement containing ephedrine, has caused one death by stroke. Ma huang is also suspected as the cause of four or five other deaths in the state. The drug requires a prescription in some states. In others, it can be purchased at a health food store.[23]

Finally, critics of prohibition point to nicotine and alcohol, which cause many deaths and accidents each year. These substances are legal. If these substances are legal, why not look at legalizing other substances?

Although there are many arguments for decriminalizing drugs, the advocates of the current policy can also make a strong case for not changing the laws against illegal drugs.

8

The Other Side— Drugs Should Not Be Legal

A majority of Americans, perhaps as many as 85 percent or more, believe that drugs should not be legal. Most support strong laws against drugs and drug use.[1] Many government and law enforcement officials agree that drugs should continue to be regulated and that those who distribute, sell, and use them should face stiff penalties.

They point to the fact that liquor consumption went up after the repeal of Prohibition. They believe that legalizing drugs would also result in an increase in drug use.

Robert DuPont, former director of the National Institute on Drug Abuse, believes that if drugs were legal, there would be 50 to 60 million regular users of cocaine and marijuana and 10 million users of heroin.[2]

Alaska and Oregon, states with the most liberal drug

97

laws, have addiction rates that are double the national average.[3]

Does drug use go up in places where the law is lenient? Let's look at some countries that softened their drug laws.

Addiction Increases When Drugs Are Legal

Spain and Italy have the highest rates of addiction and overdose in Europe. Although heroin and cocaine are legal in both countries, Spain has begun a crackdown on pushers to help decrease addiction and crime.[4]

In 1983, England changed from a program of supplying addicts with heroin through clinics to methadone treatment because the number of addicts increased 100 percent between 1970 and 1980. Many were teenagers between sixteen and seventeen years old. Even with the clinical programs, heroin addicts had a death rate twenty-six times as high as that of the average population.[5]

Switzerland decided to close a park in Zurich that had become a haven for drug users. The number of addicts living at the park went from a few hundred in 1987 to over twenty thousand in 1992 when the government shut it down because crime and prostitution had gotten out of hand.[6]

In the Netherlands, marijuana is legal and as easy to buy as ice cream. Critics of the policy point out that in Amsterdam, the capital of the Netherlands, seven thousand addicts are responsible for 80 percent of the crimes against property. Because of drugs, Amsterdam has a much larger police force than those of most American cities of a similar size.[7]

Legalization and Crime

Supporters of the current policy believe that drug-related crime would continue with legalization. They believe that people with worldwide drug interests are ruthless and will continue to deal even if drugs are legal. Some of the same dealers who traffic in heroin and cocaine are also responsible for running the multibillion-dollar business in legal drugs that are illegally sold to addicts without a prescription.

Government-run pharmacies could not compete with the illegal drug trade. Some addicts would seek out new ways to get high. It is likely that the cartels would make and sell exotic combinations of drugs such as rocks of half crack, half heroin, which have already appeared in American cities. Through black-market sales, criminals would provide addicts with what they could not get from government clinics and pharmacies.[8]

Edwin J. Delattre, a scholar in applied ethics at Boston University School of Education, argues that dealers will sell drugs twenty-four hours a day to any buyer of any age. Delattre believes that if drugs were legal, dealers would work hard to sell to young people. Even under legalization, drug use would probably still be illegal for those under twenty-one.[9] Since many hard-core drug users begin in their teens, this would ultimately produce more addicts.

Individual drug-related crime would also continue. Although some drug users are harmless, others, under the influence, behave violently. Children are often the

Police, customs agents, and agents of the DEA look at a large shipment of cocaine that has been seized in a drug bust.

innocent victims of drug-related violence. Drug Enforcement Administration agents told former drug policy administrator William Bennett about a teenage addict in New York City who sexually abused and caused permanent injuries to his one-month-old daughter while he was under the influence of crack.[10]

Prohibition of Drugs Is Not the Same as Prohibition of Alcohol

Critics of legalization believe that it is bad logic to compare prohibition of alcohol to prohibition of drugs. During Prohibition, a majority of people accepted alcoholic beverage use. Today, a majority opposes drug use. During Prohibition, it was not illegal to drink liquor; it was only illegal to sell it. World opinion also plays a part in drug control. During Prohibition, the United States was surrounded by other countries that allowed the sale of alcohol. Today, most other countries oppose drugs, and there is international agreement that drugs are dangerous. Also, today's laws against drug trafficking are more strict than were the laws against bootlegging liquor during Prohibition.[11]

The Role of Alcohol and Tobacco in the Legalization Debate

Opponents to legalization believe that comparing alcohol and tobacco to drugs like heroin, cocaine, and marijuana is like comparing apples to oranges. Cocaine and heroin are much more addictive than alcohol.[12]

Tobacco does cause many deaths, but it does not change the personality of the smoker as drugs do. A former cocaine addict described his habits:

> Everything is about getting high, and any means necessary to get there becomes rational. If it means stealing something from somebody close to you, lying to your family, borrowing money from people you know you can't pay back, writing checks you know you can't cover, you do all those things—things that are totally against everything you have ever believed in.[13]

Alcohol and tobacco do cause severe health problems, but it is difficult to argue that legalizing more dangerous substances would be justified. While prohibition did not work for alcohol because drinking was not considered morally wrong to many Americans, drug prohibition works because most people are against drug use.

Perhaps if more had been known about tobacco and alcohol years ago, they would have been more tightly regulated as addictive substances. Actually, there is a trend around the world to tighten controls on these substances. Alcohol is now illegal in several countries— about 20 percent of the world's population. Smoking is also on a decline, and in many parts of the United States it is illegal to smoke in public.[14]

Marijuana Should Not Be Legalized

Marijuana is the most widely used illegal drug in the United States. Statistics from the National Institute on Drug Abuse show that 38.2 percent of the class of 1994 tried marijuana, compared to 5.9 percent who had tried cocaine. It also appears that marijuana use among high school students is increasing slightly.[15]

Those in favor of prohibition believe that marijuana is a habit-forming drug that is particularly dangerous to young users. Studies have shown that pot smoking affects the ability to learn.[16]

Between 1965 and 1970, when many young middle-class Americans were smoking marijuana, psychiatrists Harold Kolansky and William Moore studied thirty pot smokers between the ages of thirteen and twenty-four who smoked at least twice a week but did not use other drugs. Their symptoms included poor attention span, poor concentration, confusion, anxiety, depression, apathy, and slow or slurred speech.[17]

Marijuana can affect judgment, critics say. Some

researchers have linked pot smoking to homicide. It was reported to be the most common illegal drug used by 268 murderers in New York State prisons in 1984. One third of the prisoners had used marijuana the day before the homicide, and three quarters said they experienced an effect from the drug when the murder occurred. Many of the murderers interviewed said that they felt their marijuana use was a factor in their crimes. Because the marijuana being sold today is much stronger, its effects may be more extreme.

Critics of legalizing marijuana also believe that the drug creates serious health problems. Pot contains fifty to one hundred times more cancer-causing chemicals than tobacco smoke, and cases of cancer have been reported in young users, including cancer of the tongue, mouth, larynx, jaw, head, neck, and lungs. Babies born to heavy marijuana users have a higher chance of developing leukemia, a form of cancer that attacks the blood.[18]

Critics also argue that marijuana is a gateway drug that leads to using other, more dangerous substances. Although not all marijuana users go on to use other drugs, almost everyone who does use hard drugs used marijuana first.

Legalization of Drugs for Medical Use

Many supporters of legalization believe that marijuana and heroin should be available for medical treatment. Heroin, they say, is a more powerful painkiller than morphine. In addition to helping control glaucoma, marijuana is helpful in treating the side effects of chemotherapy in cancer patients.

Currently, the DEA has not allowed marijuana to be used medically because there are good arguments against its use. Studies that back up the effectiveness of THC in glaucoma treatment were not conducted using marijuana. Instead, they used THC, which had been extracted from the plant. To get the same effect from marijuana, a glaucoma patient would have to smoke so much that he or she would be stoned all day. Although the marijuana might help reduce pressure in the eye, it can also cause complications by decreasing the user's blood pressure, reducing the blood supply to the optic nerve.

Other medical uses for marijuana are also disputed. The National Cancer Institute has concluded that marijuana is not particularly helpful in controlling the side effects of chemotherapy. When used to treat the effects of AIDS, marijuana damages the immune system and makes patients more likely to get sick from colds and viruses. Because crude marijuana contains over 420 other dangerous substances, it also increases the danger of developing cancer.[19]

Allowing heroin to be used to help control cancer pain is also questionable. Although heroin stops pain quickly, it wears off more rapidly than morphine.

Making heroin available by prescription would also be a dangerous practice because it would increase the likelihood that addicts would break into pharmacies to steal the drug. It is estimated that 50 percent of current drugstore burglaries are by addicts who are trying to steal controlled substances.[20]

Opponents to decriminalization for medical use are often opposed to providing needle exchanges as a way to cut down on the spread of AIDS and other diseases. They fear that handing out needles without a prescription undermines antidrug campaigns aimed at young people. In Los Angeles, opponents claim that needle exchanges bring addicts into a neighborhood, where they steal property and leave the sidewalks strewn with trash. California's governor, Pete Wilson, has twice vetoed legislation that would have established pilot programs to hand out needles without prescriptions.[21]

Legalization Would Not Save Taxpayer Money

Fighting drug addiction is very expensive, but legalization would be even more costly because there would probably be an increase in the number of addicts with health problems. Taxes would have to be raised for treatment programs, and health insurance premiums would probably rise sharply.

For example, in 1988, it cost $2.5 billion to provide intensive care for crack babies. For those children who survive, it will cost $15 billion to prepare them for kindergarten, and then between $6 and $12 billion a year to provide special education. The cost of educating the crack babies born during 1988 will probably be approximately $90 billion before they graduate from college.

In 1987, a study showed that drug addicts cost the country about $33 million in job-related accidents and loss of productivity. If the addiction rate increases, the amount could go as high as $210 billion a year.

Supporters of legalization say that if drugs could be taxed, they would provide money for the government; however, it is not likely that the amount raised could come close to the cost of increased addiction.[22]

Legalization Would Not Solve the Drug Problem

Those who support keeping drugs illegal agree that the current policy does have problems. They realize that law enforcement cannot entirely control drug use and addiction. They realize that the drug problem will continue as long as there is a demand for drugs. Still, they believe that strict laws and continued vigilance on the part of law enforcement are the best ways to handle the drug problem.

Lee Brown, director of National Drug Control Policy in the Clinton administration, said, "given what the overwhelming number of Americans want, and given what we have to do to address the terrible consequences of drug use, legalization is a marginal issue. It does not get to the core of the problem. In seeking to satisfy the few, it subverts the best interests of the many."[23]

9

Treatment and Education Can Help Solve the Problem

When Dawn was fourteen, she took her first drink to feel like a part of the "in" crowd. Before long she was using pills, marijuana, speed, and then heroin and cocaine. The time between her first drink and her first snort was only about eighteen months.

She drank and did drugs for almost twenty years before going into treatment in a twelve-step program of recovery, but after a year of abstinence she became ill and started taking drugs again. After landing in jail, she signed herself into a mental institution, ready to begin treatment in earnest. She learned that she was not a bad person, but a sick person.

"For me there is no shame in being a recovering addict," Dawn writes. "I know there are worse things in this world I can be: namely, an active addict. Today I realize I will die *with* my disease, but I don't have to die *of* it."[1]

Getting serious about treating her drug problem probably saved Dawn's life.

Almost everyone agrees that the real solution to the drug problem is reducing the demand for illegal substances. "If you talk to Federal officials now, versus eight years ago, more will agree that you can't prosecute your way out of this [the drug problem]. Treatment and prevention have to equal law enforcement," said Mayor Kurt L. Schmoke of Baltimore in 1995.[2]

For years the debate over the use of treatment as a tool in solving the drug problem has revolved around the question of whether drug abuse is a crime or an illness.

Even before drugs became illegal, some addicts turned to clinics or sanitariums for help. By 1910, there were probably more than a hundred treatment facilities in the United States.[3]

When Congress strengthened the Harrison Act in 1919 to stop doctors from prescribing drugs to help addicts maintain their habit, a special report was issued which declared that opium addiction had a disease aspect. In April 1919, several New York City doctors and pharmacists were arrested for supplying addicts with drugs. The next morning, April 10, a narcotic supply clinic opened to supply addicts with low-cost maintenance drugs. Twelve addicts came the first day; the second day 135 came. This was the first of a number of government-run maintenance clinics.

Between 1919 and 1921, there were approximately forty municipal treatment facilities. The clinics were not popular with drug prohibitionists because many addicts seemed more interested in obtaining cheap drugs than in a long-term cure. By 1921, the clinics were considered a failure.[4]

In the 1920s, the government decided that attacking

In the 1920s, federal drug treatment facilities resembled prisons.

the supply of drugs and drug use through law enforcement was the best way to control the drug problem.[5] Since that time, government funding for treatment has had its ups and downs. Although residential treatment programs cost about half as much as putting drug abusers in prison, more money is budgeted for prisons than for treatment.

In 1990, Phoenix House, a nonprofit treatment program that has six sites in New York and four in California, cost about forty dollars a day for each adult. (Care for teens might have been even more expensive because their treatment may last for a longer period of time. Adults who have to return to work may have a shorter therapy period. The length of treatment may also be determined by health insurance coverage.) Treating an addict in a federal prison cost the taxpayers about sixty-eight dollars a day.[6]

Successful treatment has other savings. A California study found that in 1992, the cost of drug treatment for the approximately 150,000 users in that state was $209 million. The amount saved that year and the next was 1.5 billion. The main reason for the saving was the decrease in drug-related crime.[7]

According to the RAND Corporation, a research organization in California, the taxpayers saved seven dollars for every dollar invested in drug treatment in 1992. The savings came because people use fewer drugs and less alcohol after treatment. This, in turn lowers the costs of crime and health care.[8]

Opponents to spending vast amounts of public funds for treatment argue that government-funded programs do not stop drug abuse because many addicts drop out and the majority who stay return to using drugs.

Only half of the cocaine addicts who enter treatment stay clean of drugs for up to two years. Seventy percent of these also have mental problems or problems with alcohol.[9]

"If the country wants to get serious, like a good family it has to demand that drug users stay in treatment," says Dr. Mitch Rosenthal, director of Phoenix House.[10]

At Phoenix House, staying with treatment, a regimented combination of scheduled chores and therapy in which the addicts learn to take responsibility for their actions, is a key to success. Although about half of the drug abusers who start the Phoenix House program drop out, most of the thirty thousand who have completed the eighteen-to twenty-four-month program since 1967 have managed to turn their lives around.[11]

Drug addiction is a lifetime fight, and there is no known treatment that works 100 percent of the time. Spending large amounts of money on treatment takes away from the money that could be spent on law enforcement, critics say. They also point out that not all the slots in federally funded programs are filled. They say that few addicts voluntarily go into treatment. Most wait until they are pressured by law enforcement, an employer, or their families.[12]

Those who support federally funded treatment clinics point to the fact that there are waiting lists for treatment in urban areas like Los Angeles, New York, and Miami. Private treatment is very expensive. In 1990, it was estimated that treatment at private clinics could run as high as thirty-five thousand dollars for in-patient care. Because insurance only covers about twenty-eight days of treatment, when coverage runs out, even middle-class addicts turn to public programs, creating additional demand.[13]

Public programs are usually crowded. In 1995, it was estimated that 2.4 million of the estimated 3.8 million users of illegal drugs could benefit from a drug treatment program. Unfortunately, there was only room to treat about 1.4 million users. An addict may have to wait for weeks or even months for treatment even though he or she would like to break the drug habit. Waiting can make a difference between recovery and failure.[14]

As long as there is an appetite for drugs, there will be a market in illegal substances. An important key to solving the drug problem is to reduce the demand for drugs. Local leaders, teachers, parents, law enforcement, the religious community, and young people themselves realize that drug prevention and education are the best way to fight drug abuse at the community level. Programs such as the Partnership for a Drug-Free America, Drug Abuse Resistance Education (D.A.R.E.), Parents Resources Institute on Drug Education (PRIDE), and the American Council for Drug Education have had an impact on many people's decision not to use drugs. These organizations focus on education through school programs, parent workshops, and community programs.

Annual surveys by PRIDE show that parents and school involvement can dramatically lower drug use by teens. Young people whose parents discuss drug problems with them are less likely to use drugs than are those whose parents never talk about drugs.

Drug prevention programs in schools are also effective. In Kansas City, Missouri, sixth and seventh graders receive classroom training in drug resistance and the problems of using cigarettes, alcohol, and marijuana, which are considered pathways to more serious drug use. Follow-up studies show that these students use drugs only half as much as typical students in their age group.[15]

Unfortunately, though, there probably will always be some people who will try drugs—and the debate over how to deal with substance abuse, use, and drug trafficking will continue.

The issue raises many questions with few easy answers. Are drug abusers criminals or are they people who have an illness? Should adults in a free society have an absolute right to decide whether or not to use drugs?

112

Education also plays a role in stopping the demand for drugs. Bumper stickers such as this one from the Los Angeles Sheriff's Department are one way to raise public awareness about the problems of drugs.

Are mandatory minimum sentences a good way to control illegal drug use or do they violate a person's constitutional right to be protected against unjust imprisonment? Does a school or employer have the right to demand random drug tests or are these a violation of the Fourth Amendment, which forbids unreasonable search and seizure? Should scarce government funds be used to treat drug abusers or should they be spent on law enforcement? Should sick people who might benefit from marijuana be allowed to use it legally? Should some or all drugs be legalized for personal use or should they remain illegal? Should billions of dollars be spent to fight drugs locally, nationally, and internationally?

These are some of the questions that will be debated in the years ahead as lawmakers and citizens try to deal with the problem of drugs. What do you think about the serious questions surrounding the issue of legalizing drugs?

Chapter Notes

Chapter 1

1. David G. Savage, "High Court OKs Routine Testing of Students for Drugs," *The Los Angeles Times,* June 27, 1995, p. A1.

2. *Facts about Alcohol and Other Drug Use among Children and Teens* (Washington, D.C.: The American Council for Drug Education, n.d.), p. 1.

3. "America's War on Drugs—Searching for Solutions," transcript, *ABC News,* March 28, 1995, Journal Graphics, Inc., p. 5.

4. Kurt L. Schmoke, "Back to the Future," *The Humanist,* September/October 1990, p. 29.

5. "America's War on Drugs—Searching for Solutions," p. 2.

6. *Drug Legalization: Myths and Misconceptions,* U.S. Department of Justice, Drug Enforcement Administration, n.d., p. 15.

7. Sue Rusche, *Twelve Reasons Not to Legalize Drugs* (Atlanta: National Families in Action, n.d.), p. 1.

8. "America's War on Drugs—Searching for Solutions," p. 2.

Chapter 2

1. Dean Latimer and Jeff Goldberg, *Flowers in the Blood: The Story of Opium* (New York: Franklin Watts, 1981), p. 19.

2. Ibid., p. 33.

3. Brian Inglis, *The Forbidden Game: A Social History of Drugs* (New York: Charles Scribner's Sons, 1975), pp. 49–50.

4. Latimer and Goldberg, pp. 54–55.

5. H. Wayne Morgan, *Drugs in America: A Social History, 1800 –1980* (Syracuse, N.Y.: Syracuse University Press, 1981), p. 2.

6. Latimer and Goldberg, p. 67.

7. Morgan, p. 7.

8. Ibid., p. 13.

9. Ibid., pp. 13–15.

10. David F. Musto, *The American Disease* (New Haven: Yale University Press, 1973), p. 7.

11. Michael D. Lyman, *Narcotics and Crime Control* (Springfield, Ill.: Charles C. Thomas, 1987), p. 9.

12. Morgan, p. 19.

13. Musto, pp. 8–9.

14. Morgan, pp. 19–22.

15. Ibid., pp. 95–97.

16. Ibid., pp. 64–74.

17. Ibid., pp. 88–92.

18. Ibid., p. 96.

19. Susan Neiburg Terkel, *Should Drugs Be Legalized?* (New York: Franklin Watts, 1990), pp. 23–24.

20. Morgan, p. 106.

21. Terkel, pp. 24–25.

22. Morgan, pp. 99–100.

23. Latimer and Goldberg, pp. 217–219.

24. Ibid., pp. 138–144, 148–153.

25. Musto, p. 39.

26. Terkel, p. 25.

27. Ibid., pp. 26–27.

28. Musto, p. 146.

29. Ibid., pp. 131–132.

30. Ibid., pp. 183–184.

31. Morgan, pp. 119–121.

32. Ibid., p. 126.

33. Ibid., p. 127.

34. Ibid., pp. 127–128.

35. Ibid., p. 153.

36. Ibid., p. 154.

37. Terkel, p. 28.

38. Ibid., p. 29.

39. Bruce Margolin, *The Hempster's Guide to State and Federal Marijuana Laws* (Los Angeles: Just Say Know Publications, 1995), pp. 14–17.

40. Joseph D. Douglass, Jr., "The War on Drugs Should Be Prosecuted More Vigorously," in *Drug Abuse, Opposing Viewpoints,* ed. Karen L. Swisher (San Diego: Greenhaven Press, 1994), p. 59.

Chapter 3

1. *Notable School Crime and Violence Statistics,* 1994 Gallup Organization and Phi Delta Kappan 26th Gallup Poll of the Public's Attitude Toward the Public Schools, Fact Sheet, National School Safety Center (1994).

2. Cheryl Carpenter et. al., *Kids, Drugs, and Crime* (Lexington: Lexington Books, 1988), pp. 159–168.

3. *Drug-Related Crime,* Drugs & Crime Data Center & Clearinghouse, U.S. Department of Justice, Bureau of Justice Statistics, NCJ-149286, Fact Sheet, September 1994, pp. 1–2.

4. Ibid., p. 3.

5. David Ferrell, "Ruthless Ruler of the Streets," *The Los Angeles Times,* December 19, 1994, pp. A1, 20, 21.

6. Jesse Katz, "Few Get Rich, Most Struggle in Crack's Grim Economy," *The Los Angeles Times,* December 20, 1994, p. A21.

7. Ferrell, p. A21.

8. Mark Miller, "Fatal Addiction," *Mademoiselle,* November 1991, pp. 90, 180.

9. Ibid., p. 179.

10. Peter Wilkinson, "The Young and the Reckless," *Rolling Stone,* May 5, 1994, p. 32.

11. Ibid.

12. Ibid.

13. *Briefing Book,* U.S. Department of Justice, Drug Enforcement Administration Public Affairs Section, September 1992, pp. 8–9.

14. H.G. Reza, "U.S. Agents' Drug Trade Probed," *The Los Angeles Times,* June 16, 1995, pp. A3, 41.

15. Ibid.

16. Irene Sege, "The Role of Crack Babies' Environment Studied," *The Boston Globe,* May 14, 1992, pp. 1, 16.

17. Robert C. Yeager, "Kids Who Can't Say No," *Reader's Digest,* February 1991, pp. 66–71.

18. Ibid., p. 70.

19. "Monitoring the Future Study: Trends in Prevalence of Various Drugs for 8th Graders, 10th Graders, and High School Seniors" (Washington, D.C.: National Institute on Drug Abuse, December 1994), p. 4.

20. Sam Staley, "The Seriousness of Drug Abuse May be Exaggerated," in *Drug Abuse, Opposing Viewpoints*, ed. Karen L. Swisher (San Diego: Greenhaven Press, 1994), pp. 23–30.

21. Sege, pp. 1, 16.

22. Ibid., p. 16.

23. Kurt L. Schmoke, "Side Effects," *Rolling Stone*, May 5, 1994, p. 38.

24. Ethan Nadelmann and Jann S. Wenner, "Toward a Sane National Drug Policy," *Rolling Stone*, May 5, 1994, p. 26.

Chapter 4

1. Eric Schlosser, "Marijuana and the Law," *The Atlantic Monthly*, September 1994, pp. 84–86.

2. Robert C. Bonner, "Marijuana Scheduling Petition, Denial of Petition; Remand," Department of Justice Administration, Drug Enforcement Administration, 21 CFR Part 1308, March 11, 1992, pp. 20–24.

3. Michele McCormick, *Designer-Drug Abuse* (New York: Franklin Watts, 1989), p. 94.

4. Bonner, p. 24.

5. McCormick, p. 94.

6. Bonner, p. 24.

7. *Briefing Book*, U.S. Department of Justice, Drug Enforcement Administration, Public Affairs Section, September 1992, pp. 4–10.

8. Mark S. Gold, *800-Cocaine* (New York: Bantam Books, Inc., 1984), p. 5.

9. *National Narcotics Intelligence Consumers Committee (NNICC) Report, The Supply of Illicit Drugs to the United States* (Arlington, Va.: Drug Enforcement Administration, 1993), pp. 1–31.

10. *Illegal Drug Price/Purity Report, United States: January 1991–September 1994* (Arlington, Va.: Drug Enforcement Administration, March 1995), pp. 1–3.

11. "Federal Trafficking Penalties," *DEA Briefing Book*, U.S. Department of Justice, September 1992, p. 17.

12. *The NNICC Report*, pp. 32–33.

13. Charles B. Rangel, "The Killer Drug We Ignore," *The New York Times*, August 14, 1990, p. A21.

14. Mark Miller, "Fatal Addiction," *Mademoiselle*, November 1991, p. 179.

15. *The NNICC Report*, p. 35.

16. *Illegal Drug Price/Purity Report*, p. 4.

17. "Federal Trafficking Penalties," p. 17.

18. "Monitoring the Future Study: Trends in Prevalence of Various Drugs for 8th Graders, 10th Graders, and High School Seniors," (Washington, D.C.: National Institute on Drug Abuse, December 1994), pp. 1–2.

19. *The NNICC Report*, pp. 60–67.

20. Chuck Thomas, "NORML Reports . . . Citizens' Guide to Marijuana Laws," October 1994, pp. 1–4.

21. *Source to the Street, Mid-1993 Prices for Cannabis, Cocaine, Heroin* (Arlington, Va.: Drug Enforcement Agency, 1993) p. 2.

22. *The NNICC Report*, pp. 74–76.

23. Ibid., pp. 72–73.

24. Thomas H. Maugh, II, "Amphetamine Use Soars in California, Study Finds," *The Los Angeles Times*, November 29, 1995, p. A1, 18.

25. *The NNICC Report*, pp. 72–74.

26. Ibid., pp. 76–77.

27. Ibid., pp. 77–79.

28. Jonathan Harris, *Drugged Athletes: The Crisis in American Sports* (New York: Four Winds Press, 1987), pp. 90–92.

Chapter 5

1. David Bender and Bruno Leone, series eds., *Drug Trafficking: Current Controversies* (San Diego: Greenhaven Press, 1991), pp. 14–15.

2. *National Drug Control Strategy* (Washington, D.C.: Executive Office of the President, 1995), p. 14.

3. Michael D. Lyman, *Narcotics and Crime Control* (Springfield, Ill.: Charles C. Thomas, 1987), pp. 62–64.

4. *NNICC Report 1993, The Supply of Illicit Drugs to the United States* (Arlington, Va.: Drug Enforcement Administration, 1993), pp. 6–7.

5. *National Drug Control Strategy*, pp. 48–49.

6. Ibid., p. 99.

7. "International Cooperation Can Fight the Drug Trade," *National Drug Control Strategy*, September 1989, in *Drug Trafficking: Current Controversies*, (San Diego: Greenhaven Press, 1991), pp. 107–108.

8. Diana Reynolds, "The Golden Lie," *The Humanist*, September/October 1990, p. 12.

9. *National Drug Control Strategy*, pp. 99–101.

10. Doniphan Blair, "Drug War Delusions," *The Humanist*, September/October 1990, p. 7.

11. *1993 Domestic Cannabis Eradication/Suppression Program*, U.S. Department of Justice, Drug Enforcement Administration, pp. 1–4.

12. Jonathan Beaty and Richard Hornick, "A Torrent of Dirty Dollars," *Time*, December 18, 1989, pp. 50–56.

13. *Passport to Justice*, Families Against Mandatory Minimums Foundation, n.d., p. 1.

14. Eric Schlosser, "Marijuana and the Law," *The Atlantic Monthly*, September 1994, p. 86.

15. *FAMM-gram*, February-June, 1995.

Chapter 6

1. Edward M. Kennedy, "The War on Drugs Threatens Civil Liberties," *Drug Trafficking, Current Controversies* (San Diego: Greenhaven Press, 1991), pp. 57–59.

2. David G. Savage, "High Court OKs Routine Testing of Students for Drugs," *The Los Angeles Times*, June 27, 1995, pp. A1, 10.

3. *Drug Testing in the Workplace*, ACLU Briefing Paper Number 5, American Civil Liberties Union.

4. Robert L. DuPont, "Random Drug Testing in the Workplace Is Fair," in *Drug Abuse: Opposing Viewpoints*, ed. Karen L. Swisher (San Diego: Greenhaven Press, 1994), p. 125.

5. Ibid., pp. 126–127.

6. "Drop in Drug Use," *The Los Angeles Times*, April 11, 1995, p. E3.

7. Richard Willard, "Drug Testing Is Compassionate," in *Drug Abuse: Opposing Viewpoints*, ed. Karen L. Swisher (San Diego: Greenhaven Press, 1994) p. 128.

8. Craig Zwerling, James Ryan, and Endel John Orav, "The Efficacy of Preemployment Drug Screening for Marijuana and Cocaine in Predicting Employment Outcome," *Journal of the American Medical Association*, November 28, 1990, pp. 2639–2643.

9. Lester David, "Methods Used by the Military Could Reduce Drug Abuse," in *Drug Abuse: Opposing Viewpoints*, ed. Karen L. Swisher (San Diego: Greenhaven Press, 1994), p. 239.

10. "School Crime and Violence Statistical Review," *NSSC Resource Paper* (Malibu, Calif.: National School Safety Center, 1993), p. 9.

11. "Monitoring the Future Study: Trends in Prevalence of Various Drugs for 8th Graders, 10th Graders, and High School Seniors," (Washington, D.C.: National Institute on Drug Abuse, December 1994), pp. 1, 2.

12. "Nightline," commentary, ABC News, March 28, 1995.

13. David G. Savage, "Justices Consider School Drug Tests," *The Los Angeles Times*, March 29, 1995, p. A17.

14. Peter J. Howe, "Steroid Testing Proposed for High School Athletes," *The Boston Globe*, April 18, 1991, p. 38.

15. Edward F. Dolan, Jr., *Drugs in Sports* (New York: Franklin Watts, 1986), pp. 100–101.

16. David, pp. 235, 236.

17. Jacob Sullum, "A Vial Crime," *Reason*, May 1995, p. 31.

18. "Nightline," interview, ABC News, March 28, 1995.

Chapter 7

1. Francis Wilkinson, "A Separate Peace," *Rolling Stone*, May 5, 1994, p. 28.

2. Ethan Nadellman, "The Case for Legalization," *The Crisis in Drug Prohibition* (Washington, D.C.: The Cato Institute, 1990), p. 13.

3. Tom Moganthau, "Why Good Cops Go Bad," *Newsweek*, December 19, 1994, pp. 30, 31.

4. Carol Bogert and Gregory Beals, "When Cops Betray Their Community," *Newsweek*, December 19, 1994, p. 32.

5. Kurt L. Schmoke, "Back to the Future," *The Humanist*, September/October 1990, pp. 28–29.

6. David Boaz, "The Consequences of Prohibition," *The Crisis in Drug Prohibition* (Washington D.C.: The Cato Institute, 1990), p. 1.

7. Elaine Shannon, Cathy Booth, Deborah Fowler, and Michael McBride, "A Losing Battle," *Time*, December 3, 1990, p. 47.

8. Dan Weikel, "War on Crack Targets Minorities over Whites," *The Los Angeles Times*, May 21, 1995, p. A1.

9. Susan Neiburg Terkel, *Should Drugs Be Legalized?* (New York: Franklin Watts, 1990), pp. 45–46.

10. Bruce Margolin, *The Hempster's Guide to State and Federal Marijuana Laws* (Los Angeles: Just Say Know Publications, 1995), pp. 15, 16, 17.

11. Kurt L. Schmoke, "Side Effects," *Rolling Stone*, May 5, 1994, p. 38.

12. Ethan Nadelmann and Jann S. Wenner, "Toward a Sane National Drug Policy," *Rolling Stone*, May 5, 1994, p. 25.

13. Ibid.

14. Personal interview with Bruce Margolin, director of NORML, Southern California, December 1, 1995.

15. "NORML Reports . . . Citizens' Guide to Marijuana Laws," October 1994, p. 1.

16. John P. Morgan and Lynn Zimmer, "From Pothead to Crackhead?" *Newsday*, February 26, 1995, p. A36.

17. Terkel, p. 18.

18. Richard C. Paddock, "Is Smoking Pot Good Medicine?" *The Los Angeles Times*, February 26, 1995, p. A1.

19. Kim Murphy, "Arrest Sounds Alarm for Medicinal Marijuana Clubs," *The Los Angeles Times*, June 14, 1995, p. A5.

20. Dennis Romero, "Psychedelic Solutions?" *The Los Angeles Times*, November 18, 1994, pp. E1, 5.

21. Terkel, pp. 54, 55.

22. Scott Shibuya Brown, "In a Fight With a Silent Enemy," *The Los Angeles Times*, Orange County edition, April 21, 1995, p. E1.

23. Isadore Rosenfeld, "Health Report," *Vogue*, November 1994, p. 230.

Chapter 8

1. "The Legalization Issue: Should illicit drugs be available for purchase?" Committees of Correspondence handout citing statistics from the Mississippi Research Institute of Pharmaceutical Sciences.

2. Morton M. Kondracke, "Don't Legalize Drugs," *The New Republic*, June 27, 1988, pp. 16–19.

3. Richard Schwartz, "Sabotage and the War on Drugs," *Drug Awareness Information Newsletter*, in *Drug Legalization: Myths and Misconceptions*, the Seattle Field Division, A Demand Reduction Project (Arlington, Va.: Drug Enforcement Administration, 1994), p. 9.

4. Ibid., p. 26.

5. Ibid., pp. 17–19.

6. Ibid., pp. 19–20.

7. Ibid., p. 22.

8. William Bennett, "Should Drugs Be Legalized?" *Reader's Digest,* March 1990, p. 90.

9. Edwin J. Delattre, "Drugs Should Not Be Legalized," *Drug Trafficking: Current Controversies* (San Diego: Greenhaven Press, 1991), p. 83.

10. Bennett, p. 93.

11. *Drug Legalization: Myths and Misconceptions,* the Seattle Field Division, A Demand Reduction Project (Arlington, Va.: Drug Enforcement Administration, 1994), pp. 38–39.

12. Ibid., p. 36.

13. Bennett, pp. 93–94.

14. "Drug Legalization—What If?" (Baltimore: Governor's Executive Advisory Council Anti-Legalization Panel, 1994), p. 7.

15. "Monitoring the Future Study, 1975–1994, National High School Senior Drug Abuse Survey," (Washington, D.C.: National Institute on Drug Abuse, 1994).

16. "Low doses of THC found to cause learning deficits," *Marijuana Research Review, Drug Watch Oregon,* January 1995, p. 1.

17. Peggy Mann, *Marijuana Alert* (New York: McGraw-Hill, 1985), p. 217.

18. "Marijuana: More Harmful than You Think," Committees of Correspondence, Inc., Drug Prevention Resources, October 1994.

19. *Drug Legalization: Myths and Misconceptions,* p. 47.

20. Ibid., p. 51.

21. Jack Cheevers, "Few Needle Swaps Exist as HIV Spreads in L.A. County," *The Los Angeles Times,* January 9, 1995, p. A1.

22. *Drug Legalization: Myths and Misconceptions,* pp. 45–53.

23. "Drug Legalization–What If?" p. 11.

Chapter 9

1. Dawn M. Martin, "I'm Dawn, and I'm an Addict," *Essence,* September 1994, p. 46.

2. Michael Janofsky, "Baltimore Grapples with Idea of Legalizing Drugs," *The New York Times*, April 20, 1995, p. A8.

3. H. Wayne Morgan, *Drugs in America: A Social History, 1800–1980* (Syracuse, N.Y.: Syracuse University Press, 1981), p. 74.

4. David F. Musto, *The American Disease: Origins of Narcotic Control* (New Haven, Conn.: Yale University Press, 1973), pp. 141, 151, 152.

5. Ibid., p. 181.

6. Laurie Kretchmar, "Up from the Ashes at Phoenix House," *Fortune*, March 12, 1990, p. 78.

7. *National Drug Control Strategy* (Washington, D.C.: Executive Office of the President, 1995), p. 38.

8. Ibid., p. 55.

9. Louis Kraar, "How to Win the War on Drugs," *Fortune*, March 12, 1990, p. 71.

10. Ibid.

11. Kretchmar, p. 78.

12. Jeffery A. Eisenach and Andrew J. Corwin, "Increasing Federal Funding for Treatment Programs Will Not Reduce Drug Abuse," in *Drug Abuse: Opposing Viewpoints*, ed. Karen L. Swisher (San Diego: Greenhaven Press, 1994), pp. 216–224.

13. George M. Anderson, "Increasing Federal Funding for Treatment Programs Will Reduce Drug Abuse," in *Drug Abuse: Opposing Viewpoints*, pp. 210–211.

14. *National Drug Control Strategy*, pp. 38–39.

15. Kraar, p. 74.

Glossary

addiction—Physical or psychological dependence on a substance.

amphetamines—Pills taken to give the user energy. They should be taken only when prescribed.

barbiturates—Addictive drugs that depress the central nervous system.

cartel—A group of drug traffickers who illegally produce and sell drugs.

casual use—Occasional use of a drug without becoming addicted to it.

China White—A designer drug similar to heroin that has claimed many deaths and overdoses. It can cause symptoms similar to those of Hodgkin's disease, ranging from partial paralysis to death.

cocaine—A drug made from the leaves of the coca plant. The chemical name is cocaine hydrochloride. The drug is an extremely powerful stimulant.

controlled drugs—Since 1970, drugs of abuse have been divided into five schedules of categories. Use of these drugs is controlled by the Drug Enforcement Administration.

courier—A person who takes a shipment of drugs from one country to another or from one state to another.

crack—A very addictive form of cocaine with a high potency and relatively low street price.

designer drugs—Chemicals that provide a high similar to the high produced by controlled drugs. These are usually made in underground labs and may differ slightly from other illegal drugs in their chemical makeup.

detoxification—The process of removing drugs from a user's system during treatment. It involves abstaining from drug use.

drug rehabilitation—The process that helps a user get off drugs. It includes removing the drug from his or her system and providing psychological counseling to help the user understand the reasons for taking drugs.

Ecstasy—A designer drug, also known as MDMA, that appeared around 1985 and that has some of the effects of LSD without the flashbacks or bad trips. It is popular at all-night dance parties called raves.

eradication—Destroying crops of plants that produce drugs.

euphoria—A sense of well-being or a mental high.

freebasing—A way of taking cocaine to achieve an intense high.

hallucination—An impression of sights and sounds that are not actually present. Hallucinations may be drug induced.

hallucinogen—A drug such as LSD which causes hallucinations.

hashish—A drug made from the resins of the marijuana plant.

heroin—An opiate which is produced from morphine.

huffing—Inhaling the fumes of household substances such as paint, hair spray, or gasoline.

inhalants—Substances that are inhaled or "huffed."

interdiction—Stopping drugs from crossing international borders to come into the United States.

LSD (Lysergic Acid Diethylamide)—A hallucinogenic drug, especially popular in the 1960s and 1970s. It comes from a fungus that grows on morning glory seeds or rye.

mandatory minimum sentences—A minimum sentence that must be given for possession of and dealing in a given amount of an illegal drug.

marijuana—A drug that comes from the hemp plant, called cannabis sativa. The active ingredient in marijuana is THC. It is also called pot.

mescaline—A hallucinogenic drug found in peyote cactus.

methadone—A synthetic narcotic given to heroin addicts to satisfy their craving for the drug without the drug's effects. It does not produce the side effects of heroin.

methamphetamine—A white or off-white powder that is similar to amphetamine. It is a powerful stimulant. Often the drug is distributed through outlaw motorcycle gangs.

morphine—A derivative of the opium poppy that is used as a painkiller. It was developed in 1803 as a cure for opium addiction.

narcotic—Substance that is a sedative or that produces a state of sleep. Sometimes the term is used to refer to any substance that causes dependence.

nicotine—The addictive substance in tobacco.

opiate—Any drug that comes from the juice of the opium poppy, including opium, morphine, codeine, and heroin.

opium—A sedative drug that comes from the juice of the opium poppy.

paraphernalia—Equipment used to take or store illegal drugs.

psychedelic drug—A drug that causes hallucinations or changes sense perceptions.

snorting—The usual method of taking cocaine or certain other drugs. The user lays out "lines" on a smooth surface, inhaling the drug one line at a time through rolled-up paper or from the bowl of a spoon.

stimulant—A substance that speeds up the reactions of the central nervous system.

withdrawal—Physical and emotional symptoms a user feels when he or she stops taking drugs or drinking alcohol.

Further Reading

Bender, David, and Bruno Leone, editors. *Drug Abuse, Opposing Viewpoints.* San Diego: Greenhaven Press, Inc., 1994.

Bender, David L. *Drug Trafficking, Current Controversies.* San Diego: Greenhaven Press, Inc., 1991.

Carroll, Marilyn. *PCP, The Encyclopedia of Psychoactive Drugs.* New York: Chelsea House Publishers, 1985.

Johnson, Joan J. *America's War on Drugs.* New York: Franklin Watts, 1990.

Mann, Peggy. *Marijuana Alert.* New York: McGraw-Hill, 1985.

Oglesby, E.W., Samuel J. Faber, and Stuart J. Faber. *Angel Dust: What Everyone Should Know About PCP.* Los Angeles: Lega-Books, 1979.

Terkel, Susan Neiburg. *Should Drugs Be Legalized?* New York: Franklin Watts, 1990.

Index

127